StartUp

Ken Beatty, Series Consultant

5

Jenifer Edens
Genevieve Kocienda
Linda L. Lane
Paul MacIntyre
Jenni Currie Santamaria
Geneva Tesh

StartUp 5

Copyright © 2019 by Pearson Education, Inc.

All rights reserved. No part of this publication may be reproduced, stored in a retrieval system, or transmitted in any form or by any means, electronic, mechanical, photocopying, recording, or otherwise, without the prior permission of the publisher.

Pearson, 221 River Street, Hoboken, NJ 07030

Staff credits: The people who made up the StartUp team representing editorial, production, and design are Pietro Alongi, Héctor González Álvarez, Gregory Bartz, Peter Benson, Magdalena Berkowska, Stephanie Callahan, Jennifer Castro, Tracey Munz Cataldo, Dave Dickey, Gina DiLillo, Irene Frankel, Sarah Henrich, Christopher Leonowicz, Bridget McLaughlin, Kamila Michalak, Laurie Neaman, Alison Pei, Jennifer Raspiller, Jeremy Schaar, Katherine Sullivan, Stephanie Thornton, Paula Van Ells, and Joseph Vella.

Cover credit: Front cover: Javier Osores/EyeEm/Getty Images. Back cover: Klaus Vedfelt/Getty Images (Level 1); Alexandre Moreau/Getty Images (Level 2); Matteo Colombo/Getty Images (Level 3); Javier Osores/EyeEm/Getty Images (Level 4); Liyao Xie/Getty Images (Level 5); Ezra Bailey/Getty Images (Level 6); guvendemir/Getty Images (Level 7); Yusuke Shimazu/EyeEm/Getty Images (Level 8); tovovan/Shutterstock (icons)

Text composition: emc design ltd

Library of Congress cataloging-in-publication data on file.

Photo and illustration credits: See pages 166–167

Printed in the United States of America

ISBN-10: 0-13-468419-2

ISBN-13: 978-0-13-468419-2

ISBN-10: 0-13-517842-8 (with app and Online Practice)

ISBN-13: 978-0-13-517842-3 (with app and Online Practice)

1 2019

ACKNOWLEDGMENTS

We would like to thank the following people for their insightful and helpful comments and suggestions.

Maria Alam, Extension Program-Escuela Americana, San Salvador, El Salvador; **Milton Ascencio**, Universidad Don Bosco, Soyapango, El Salvador; **Raul Avalos**, CALUSAC, Guatemala City, Guatemala; **Adrian Barnes**, Instituto Chileno Norteericano, Santiago, Chile; **Laura Bello**, Centro de Idiomas Xalapa, Universidad Veracruzana, Xalapa, México; **Jeisson Alonso Rodriguez Bonces**, Fort Dorchester High School, Bogotá, Colombia; **Juan Pablo Calderón Bravo**, Manpower English, Santiago, Chile; **Ellen J. Campbell**, RMIT, Ho Chi Minh City, Vietnam; **Vinicio Cancinos**, CALUSAC, Guatemala City, Guatemala; **Viviana Castilla**, Centro de Enseñanza de Lenguas Extranjeras UN, México; **Bernal Cespedes**, ULACIT, Tournón, Costa Rica; **Carlos Celis**, Cel. Lep Idiomas S.A., São Paulo, Brazil; **Carlos Eduardo Aguilar Cortes**, Universidad de los Andes, Bogotá, Colombia; **Solange Lopes Vinagre Costa**, Senac-SP, São Paulo, Brazil; **Isabel Cubilla**, Panama Bilingüe, Panama City, Panama; **Victoria Dieste**, Alianza Cultural Uruguay-Estados Unidos, Montevideo, Uruguay; **Francisco Domerque**, Georgal Idiomas, México City, México; **Vern Eaton**, St. Giles International, Vancouver, Canada; **Maria Fajardo**, Extension Program-Escuela Americana, San Salvador, El Salvador; **Diana Elizabeth Leal Ffrench**, Let's Speak English, Cancún, México; **Rosario Giraldez**, Alianza Cultural Uruguay-Estados Unidos, Montevideo, Uruguay; **Lourdes Patricia Rodríguez Gómez**, Instituto Tecnológico de Chihuahua, Chihuahua, México; **Elva Elizabeth Martínez de González**, Extension Program-Escuela Americana, San Salvador, El Salvador; **Gabriela Guel**, Centro de Idiomas de la Normal Superior, Monterrey, México; **Ana Raquel Fiorani Horta**, SENAC, Ribeirão Preto, Brazil; **Carol Hutchinson**, Heartland International English School, Winnipeg, Canada; **Deyanira Solís Juárez**, Centro de Idiomas de la Normal Superior, Monterrey, México; **Miriam de Käppel**, Colegio Bilingüe El Prado, Guatemala City, Guatemala; **Ikuko Kashiwabara**, Osaka Electro-Communication University, Neyagawa, Japan; **Steve Kirk**, Nippon Medical School, Tokyo, Japan; **Jill Landry**, GEOS Languages Plus, Ottawa, Canada; **Tiffany MacDonald**, East Coast School of Languages, Halifax, Canada; **Angélica Chávez Escobar Martínez**, Universidad de León, León, Guanajuato, México; **Renata Martinez**, CALUSAC, Guatemala City, Guatemala; **Maria Alejandra Mora**, Keiser International Language Institute, San Marcos, Carazo, Nicaragua; **Alexander Chapetón Morales**, Abraham Lincoln School, Bogotá, Colombia; **José Luis Castro Moreno**, Universidad de León, León, Guanajuato, México; **Yukari Naganuma**, Eikyojuku for English Teachers, Tokyo, Japan; **Erina Ogawa**, Daito Bunka University, Tokyo, Japan; **Carolina Zepeda Ortega**, Let's Speak English, Cancún, México; **Lynn Passmore**, Vancouver International College, Vancouver, Canada; **Noelle Peach**, EC English, Vancouver, Canada; **Ana-Marija Petrunic**, George Brown College, Toronto, Canada; **Romina Planas**, Centro Cultural Paraguayo Americano, Asunción, Paraguay; **Sara Elizabeth Portela**, Centro Cultural Paraguayo Americano, Asunción, Paraguay; **Luz Rey**, Centro Colombo Americano, Bogotá, Colombia; **Ana Carolina González Ramírez**, Universidad de Costa Rica, San José, Costa Rica; **Octavio Garduno Ruiz**, AIPT Service S.C., Coyoacán, México; **Amado Sacalxot**, Colegio Lehnsen Americas, Guatemala City, Guatemala; **Deyvis Sanchez**, Instituto Cultural Dominico-Americano, Santo Domingo, Dominican Republic; **Lucy Slon**, JFK Adult Centre, Montreal, Canada; **Scott Stulberg**, University of Regina, Regina, Canada; **Maria Teresa Suarez**, Colegios APCE, San Salvador, El Salvador; **Daniel Valderrama**, Centro Colombo Americano, Bogotá, Colombia; **Kris Vicca**, Feng Chia University, Taichung, Taiwan; **Sairy Matos Villanueva**, Centro de Actualización del Magisterio, Chetumal, Q.R., México; **Edith Espino Villarreal**, Universidad Tecnológica de Panama, El Dorado, Panama; **Isabela Villas Boas**, Casa Thomas Jefferson, Brasília, Brazil

LEARNING OBJECTIVES

Pronunciation	Reading	Writing	Presentation
• Linking vowels with /w/ and /y/	• Read about a wildlife rescue center Skill Find the main idea	• Write a description of a place Skill Use sensory words	• Give a presentation about an endangered animal Skill Use comparisons for measurements
• Stress in compound adjectives	• Read about job satisfaction Skill Understand rhetorical questions	• Write about making a change Skill Use linking expressions	• Give a presentation about a job you were interested in when you were a child Skill Practice by listening to recordings of yourself
• Phrases with of	• Read a TV review Skill Construct mental images	• Write about local events Skill Categorize	• Give a presentation about a festival in another country Skill Use pauses
• The prefix ex-	• Read about important possessions Skill Link the past to the present	• Write a complaint Skill Use polite language	• Give a presentation about a new store Skill Show enthusiasm
• Blending phrases with so and neither	• Read about the habits of top athletes Skill Notice concluding sentences	• Write about bad habits Skill Use a hook	• Give a presentation about home remedies Skill Use large visual aids

Unit	Vocabulary	Grammar	Conversation / Speaking	Listening
6 Has the criminal been caught? **page 65**	• Crime and criminals • The legal process	• Past perfect • Present perfect passive • *Do / did* as a verb substitute	• Describe a crime • Talk about law and order • Discuss crime-solving technology Skill Keep your listener interested	• Listen to a talk about advances in forensic technology Skill Listen for contrasts
7 Did you see what she's wearing? **page 77**	• Verbs related to clothing • Adjectives to describe clothing • Clothing repair	• Reduced defining relative clauses • Passive causatives • *Would rather (than)*	• Talk about people's clothes • Talk about clothing repairs • Discuss fashion and attitude Skill Accept compliments	• Listen to a talk about how clothing affects your attitude Skill Listen for opinions
8 Do I need to install something? **page 89**	• Technology • Using software	• *Wish / If only* to express regrets • Showing purpose • *Even* to emphasize a point	• Talk about regrets • Describe using a computer • Discuss social media and friendship Skill Respond to gratitude	• Listen to a talk about social media and friendship Skill Listen for sources
9 Are you ready to walk away? **page 101**	• People at a conference • Verbs for negotiating	• Causative verbs: *get, have,* and *make* • Advice, obligation, and expectation • *Unless*	• Talk about a past negotiation • Negotiate a deal • Discuss negotiation skills Skill End a phone call	• Listen to a talk about how negotiating is like dancing Skill Listen for comparisons
10 How's she doing? **page 113**	• Explaining and arguing • Interacting with others	• Embedded *yes / no* questions • Questions with final prepositions • Repeated and parallel comparatives	• Talk about a conversation • Discuss a difficult interaction • Discuss dealing with difficult people Skill Accept an apology	• Listen to a talk about dealing with difficult people Skill Listen for words that signal importance

Pronunciation	Reading	Writing	Presentation
• The letters -se	• Read about Sherlock Holmes Skill Identify examples	• Write about a crime Skill Use the 5 Ws and *how*	• Give a presentation about criminals who made mistakes Skill Make eye contact
• Emphatic stress	• Read about a fashion designer Skill Identify reasons	• Write about personal style Skill Express opinions	• Give a presentation about how appearances can be deceiving Skill Use notes
• Contractions of the auxiliary *had*	• Read about a high-tech city Skill Recognize bias	• Write about a new technology Skill Explain a problem and solution	• Give a presentation about favorite apps and websites Skill Use charts
• *Have to, has to, had better (not)*	• Read about negotiating styles Skill Make inferences	• Write about a conflict Skill Explain different points of view	• Give a presentation about developing confidence for negotiations Skill Use a loud, clear voice
• Linking verbs to prepositions	• Read about extreme altruism Skill Identify paraphrasing	• Write about a kindness Skill Use past tenses to show sequence	• Give a presentation about someone you appreciate Skill End your presentation positively

Key

▶00-00 audio   ▶ video   discussion   presentation self-evaluation

abc flashcards   ActiveTeach   🔍 web search

TO THE TEACHER

Welcome to StartUp

StartUp is an innovative eight-level, general American English course for adults and young adults who want to make their way in the world and need English to do it. The course takes students from CEFR A1 to C1 and enables teachers and students to track their progress in detail against the Global Scale of English (GSE) Learning Objectives.

StartUp Level	GSE Range	CEFR	Description	StartUp Level	GSE Range	CEFR	Description
1	22–33	A1	Beginner	5	49–58	B1+	High intermediate
2	30–37	A2	High beginner	6	56–66	B2	Upper intermediate
3	34–43	A2+	Low intermediate	7	64–75	B2+	Low advanced
4	41–51	B1	Intermediate	8	73–84	C1	Advanced

English for 21st century learners

StartUp helps your students develop the spoken and written language they need to communicate in their personal, academic, and work lives. In each lesson, you help students build the collaborative and critical thinking skills so essential for success in the 21st century. *StartUp* allows students to learn the language in ways that work for them: anytime anywhere. The Pearson Practice English App allows students to access their English practice on the on the go. Additionally, students have all the audio and video files at their fingertips in the app and on the Pearson English Portal.

Personalized, flexible teaching

The unit structure and the wealth of support materials give you options to personalize the class to best meet your students' needs. *StartUp* gives you the freedom to focus on different strands and skills; for example, you can spend more class time on listening and speaking. You can choose to teach traditionally or flip the learning. You can teach sections of the lesson in the order you prefer. And you can use the ideas in the Teacher's Edition to help you extend and differentiate instruction, particularly for mixed-ability and for large and small classes.

Motivating and relevant learning

StartUp creates an immersive learning experience with a rich blend of multimedia videos and interactive activities, including interactive flashcards for vocabulary practice; Grammar Coach and Pronunciation Coach videos; interactive grammar activities; podcasts, interviews, and other audio texts for listening practice; humorous, engaging videos with an international cast of characters for modeling conversations; high-interest video talks beginning at Level 5; media project videos in Levels 1–4 and presentation skills videos in Levels 5–6 for end-of-unit skills consolidation.

Access at your fingertips

StartUp provides students with everything they need to extend their learning to their mobile device. The app empowers students to take charge of their learning outside of class, allowing them to practice English whenever and wherever they want, online or offline. The app provides practice of vocabulary, grammar, listening, and conversation. Students can go to any lesson by scanning a QR code on their Student Book page or through the app menu. The app also provides students with access to all the audio and video files from the course.

Components

For the Teacher

StartUp provides everything you need to plan, teach, monitor progress, and assess learning.

The *StartUp ActiveTeach* front-of-class tool allows you to

- zoom in on the page to focus the class's attention
- launch the vocabulary flashcard decks from the page
- use tools, like a highlighter, to emphasize specific text
- play all the audio texts and videos from the page
- pop up interactive grammar activities
- move easily to and from any cross-referenced pages

The interleaved *Teacher's Edition* includes

- an access code to the Pearson Practice English App and all digital resources
- language and culture notes
- teaching tips to help you improve your teaching practice
- *look for* notes to help assess students' performance
- answer keys to all Student Book exercises on the facing page of the notes
- and more!

Teacher's Digital Resources, all available on the Pearson English Portal, include

- Teacher Methodology Handbook
- A unit walkthrough
- ActiveTeach front-of-class software
- ExamView assessment software
- Teacher's notes for every Student Book page
- Rubrics for speaking and writing
- Hundreds of reproducible worksheets
- Answer keys for all practice
- Audio and video scripts
- The GSE Teacher Mapping Booklet
- The GSE Toolkit

For the Student

StartUp provides students with everything they need to extend their learning.

The optional *MyEnglishLab for StartUp* gives students more formal online practice and provides immediate feedback, hints, and tips. It includes

- grammar practice with access to all the Grammar Coach videos
- vocabulary practice, including games and flashcards
- speaking and pronunciation activities, including access to all the conversation videos and Pronunciation Coach videos
- listen-and-record practice that lets students record themselves and compare their recordings to models
- auto-graded reading and writing practice that reinforces skills taught in the Student Book
- summative assessments that measure students' mastery of listening, vocabulary, grammar, pronunciation, and reading
- a gradebook, which records scores on practice and assessments, that both students and you can use to help monitor progress and plan further practice

The optional *StartUp Workbook* provides practice of vocabulary, grammar, reading, and writing and includes self-assessments of grammar and vocabulary.

WELCOME UNIT

1 IN THE CLASSROOM

A Get to know your classmates

Talk to your classmates. Find someone who matches each prompt. Write his or her first name on the line.

Find someone who…

- loves to read _____
- has ridden a horse _____
- enjoys cooking _____
- has a pet _____
- has traveled to another country _____
- is great at math _____

B Ask for help

▶00-01 Complete the conversations with sentences from the box. Then listen and check your answers.

~~Can you repeat the instructions?~~	How do you pronounce this word?
What's the difference between "advice" and "advise"?	What's the English word for "barato"?
You're saying we should do this for homework?	Could you explain that a bit more?

1. Can you repeat the instructions?
Sure. Practice the conversation with a partner.
OK.

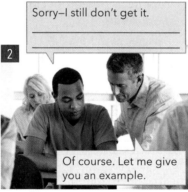

2. Sorry—I still don't get it.
_____
Of course. Let me give you an example.

3. Just to confirm—
_____
That's right.
OK. Thanks.

4. Can I ask you something?
_____
_____
The first word is a noun and the second is a verb.

5. Can you remind me—
_____
Cheap.
Oh, right. Thanks.

6. _____
_____
Repeat after me: Gorgeous.
Gorgeous.
Correct.

C ROLE PLAY Choose a conversation from 1B. Make your own conversation. Use different information.

2 LEARN ABOUT YOUR BOOK

1. Look at pages iv-vii. What information is on those pages?

   _____

2. How many units are in the book? _____

3. How many lessons are in each unit? _____

4. Where is the grammar practice? _____

5. Look at the QR code . Find the icon on page 7. What does it mean? _____

   _____

6. Look at the ☐ I CAN STATEMENT. Find it on page 11. What does it tell you? _____

   _____

7. Look at this icon 🔍. Find it on page 13. What does it mean?

   _____

3 LEARN ABOUT YOUR APP

1. Look inside the front cover. Where can you go to download the Pearson Practice English app for StartUp? _____

2. Where are the instructions for registering for the app? _____

   _____

3. Look at the picture of the app. What do you see?

   _____

4. Look at the picture again. Fill in the blanks with the numbers 1–3.
   a. Number _____ shows the practice activities.
   b. Number _____ shows the video files.
   c. Number _____ shows the audio files.

5. Look at the picture again. What does this ☁ mean? _____

6. Look at the QR code on page 7 again. What happens when you scan the code? _____

   _____

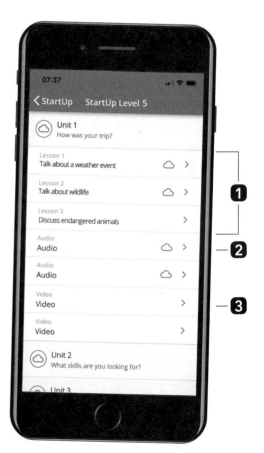

TSW MEDIA

MEET THE PEOPLE OF TSW MEDIA

To find out more, watch the videos!

TSW Media is a big company with big ideas. It has offices all over the world. It works with international clients to help them market their products and services.

LETICIA MOLINA
Photographer

▶00-02 My name is Leticia Molina, but everyone calls me Leti. I live in Santa Cruz, Bolivia. I'm a photographer.

AHMET TANIR
Illustrator

▶00-05 Hi! I'm Ahmet Tanir. I live in New Jersey with my wife and two kids. I'm an illustrator.

ED MILLER
Copywriter

▶00-03 Hi! I'm Ed Miller. I live in New York, but I'm originally from Minneapolis, Minnesota. I'm a copywriter.

MARCOS ALVES
Market Research Analyst

▶00-06 Hello. I'm Marcos Alves. I'm from São Paulo, Brazil, and I'm a market research analyst.

LAN PHAM
Event Planner

▶00-04 Hi! My name is Lan Pham. I'm from Ho Chi Minh City, in Vietnam. I'm an event planner, and I love my job.

PAULA FLOREZ
Sales Representative

▶00-07 My name is Paula Florez. I'm from Mexico City, Mexico, and I'm a sales rep.

Every year, TSW sponsors a competition for employees to get mentoring and coaching to improve their public speaking skills. Here are three of the winners!

ADRIANA LOPEZ

▶00-08 Hi. My name is Adriana Lopez. I work in the technology department in the Quito office.

KENDRICK SCOTT

▶00-09 Hey! I'm Kendrick Scott and I'm a designer in the Vancouver office.

DAVID CRUZ

▶00-10 Hi. My name is David Cruz. I'm from Florida, but I've lived and worked in Singapore for the past six years. I'm an advertising manager.

1 HOW WAS YOUR TRIP?

LEARNING GOALS

In this unit, you
⊙ talk about a weather event
⊙ talk about wildlife
⊙ discuss endangered animals
⊙ read about a wildlife rescue center
⊙ write a description of a place

GET STARTED

A Read the unit title and learning goals.

B Look at the photo. What's going on?

C Now read Leti's message. Would you like to do this?

LETI MOLINA
@LetiM

Taking pictures of wildlife in Botswana was a dream come true!

5

LETI MOLINA
@LetiM

Just got back to New York from my
photo shoot. I'm tired but happy!

 1 VOCABULARY Weather

A ▶01-01 **Listen. Then listen and repeat.**

Weather

It's pouring.   It's drizzling.   It's humid.

It's freezing.   It's hailing.   It's overcast.

Results of bad weather

get soaked   get sunburned

get damaged   get stuck

B ▶01-02 **Listen. Circle the correct word to complete the sentence.**

1. It's *drizzling* / *pouring* outside.
2. It's *drizzling* / *overcast*.
3. She got *sunburned* / *soaked*.
4. It's *humid* / *freezing* outside.
5. It's *hailing* / *overcast*.
6. His car got *stuck* / *damaged* in the storm.

C PAIRS **Talk about ways to prepare for or deal with each kind of weather in 1A.**

If it's pouring, take the subway. There are lots of car accidents in the rain.

2 GRAMMAR *Get* to express change

Use *get* + adjective or the passive with *get* to express a change of state.

Get + adjective

Subject	*Get*	Adjective	
People	**are getting**	sick	from the heat.
It	**got**	hot	after the rain stopped.

Passive with *get*

Subject	*Get*	Past participle	
The equipment	**has gotten**	damaged	by the storm.
I	**got**	soaked	in the downpour.

Commonly used with *get*

Adjectives	Participles
cold	caught
dark	confused
dirty	excited
hot	hurt
nervous	lost
thirsty	scared
wet	worried

Notes

- When *get* is followed by an adjective, it gives the idea of change or of becoming:
  People are getting sick. = People weren't sick before, but now they are beginning to be sick.
- For the passive with *get*, the past participle describes the subject.
- The passive with *get* is more common in conversation than in writing.

>> FOR PRACTICE, GO TO PAGE 125

3 CONVERSATION SKILL

A ▶01-03 Read the conversation skill. Listen. Notice that B's reply question uses a pronoun and the same verb tense as A's statement.

1. A: It's going to hail tomorrow.
   B: Is it?

2. A: I got really sunburned this weekend.
   B: Oh, no! You did?

> **Reply questions**
>
> We use reply questions to show interest and keep a conversation going. There are two ways to form these questions:
>
> | Pronoun + auxiliary verb / verb be: | Auxiliary verb / verb be + pronoun |
> |---|---|
> | You do? | Do you? |
> | She did? | Did she? |
> | He has? | Has he? |
> | They are? | Are they? |
> | It was? | Was it? |

B ▶01-04 Listen. Write a reply question.

1. _____   3. _____   5. _____
2. _____   4. _____   6. _____

4 CONVERSATION

A ▶01-05 Listen or watch. What does Leti tell Marcos about?

B ▶01-06 Listen or watch again. Write *T* (true) or *F* (false).

1. Leti saved her camera by putting it in a plastic bag. ___
2. The rain didn't last for a long time. ___
3. Leti feels disappointed about the weather on her trip. ___

> How did Leti react to the difficulties she experienced on her trip? Do you think you would react the same way? Why or why not?

C ▶01-07 FOCUS ON LANGUAGE Listen or watch. Complete the conversation.

Leti:	A couple of the people in my group _____ from the heat.
Marcos:	They did?
Leti:	Yeah, I was lucky. I _____ a little _____ , but that's it.
Marcos:	Was it humid?
Leti:	No, it was super dry.

5 TRY IT YOURSELF

A THINK Think about a time you got caught in bad weather. Complete the chart.

Where were you?	
How did the weather change?	
What did you do?	
How did you feel?	

B PAIRS Tell your partner about the weather event in 5A. Use the conversation in 4C as an example.

My friends and I were at the beach and it started getting cloudy and overcast …

C REPORT Tell the class about your partner's story. Is it similar to your story?

■ I CAN TALK ABOUT A WEATHER EVENT.

LETI MOLINA
@LetiM

I got photos of some pretty dangerous animals—but I didn't get too close!

 1 VOCABULARY Animals

A ▶01-08 **Listen. Then listen and repeat.**

FUN FACTS
about Animals!

Some bats eat 600 insects per hour.

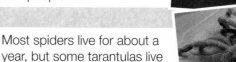
a bat

an elephant

An elephant's trunk (its long nose) is so strong that it can knock down a tree, but it can also pick up an object as tiny as a grain of rice.

The hippopotamus (hippo) spends most of its day in water, but it cannot swim or float. It always keeps its feet on the bottom of the river.

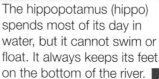
a hippopotamus (a hippo)

a lion

A lion's roar is so loud that humans can hear it from eight kilometers (five miles) away.

The blue whale is the largest animal that has ever lived on Earth. A newborn blue whale weighs as much as 100 people.

a blue whale

a snake

The smallest snake is as thin as a spaghetti noodle. The largest snake weighs more than 227 kilograms (500 pounds).

Most spiders live for about a year, but some tarantulas live for more than 20 years.

a tarantula

WORDS TO DESCRIBE ANIMALS

enormous: very large
tiny: very small
adorable: very attractive and cute
gorgeous: very beautiful

fierce: ready and able to attack
aggressive: behaving in a way that shows it wants to fight
playful: active and wanting to have fun

B Read the fun facts. Which do you find the most surprising? Tell a partner.

C PAIRS Decide together. Which animals are enormous? Tiny? Adorable? Gorgeous? Fierce? Aggressive? Playful? Take notes.

2 GRAMMAR *So and such*

Use *so* with adjectives and *such* with noun phrases to show emphasis.

		Adjective			Noun phrase
The lion is	so	**fierce.**	Hippos are	such	**dangerous animals.**
He looks		**calm.**	We had		**a good time!**

>> FOR PRACTICE, GO TO PAGE 126

3 PRONUNCIATION

A ▶01-09 Read and listen to the pronunciation note.

B ▶01-10 Listen. Notice how the two words in the examples are linked. Then listen and repeat.

Linking with /w/	Linking with /y/
so͜ʷadorable	three͜ʸ elephants
_____	_____
_____	_____
_____	_____

Linking vowels with /w/ and /y/

We often use /w/ or /y/ to link a word ending in a vowel to a word beginning with a vowel. When the first word ends in /u/, /oʊ/, or /aʊ/, use /w/ to link it to the following vowel: so͜ʷadorable, how͜ often. When the first word ends in /i/, /eɪ/, /ɔɪ/, or /aɪ/, use /y/ to link it to the following vowel: very͜ attractive, stay͜ away.

C ▶01-11 Listen. Write each phrase in the correct box in 3A. Listen and check your answers. Then listen and repeat.

1. so enormous
2. slow animals
3. baby elephants
4. free advice
5. too early
6. tiny ants

4 CONVERSATION

A ▶01-12 Listen or watch. Check (✓) the animals that they mention.

☐ elephants ☐ bats ☐ lions ☐ hippos ☐ spiders ☐ monkeys

B ▶01-13 Listen or watch again. Which animal does Leti say is …?

1. social _____
2. gorgeous _____
3. aggressive _____
4. fascinating _____

How does Leti feel about spiders? How does Marcos feel about them? Are you more like Leti or Marcos? Explain.

C ▶01-14 FOCUS ON LANGUAGE Listen or watch. Complete the conversation.

Leti:	Well, here's the first elephant I saw.
Marcos:	Wow, he's enormous!
Leti:	He's a she, actually. This is her baby.
Marcos:	Aw, he's _____ !
Leti:	He's adorable. And _____ and playful.

5 TRY IT YOURSELF

A THINK Think about a time you saw a wild animal. Write your ideas in the chart.

Animal	Where I was	Description	How I felt

B PAIRS Talk about your animal encounter. Ask questions about each other's stories.
A: I saw a lot of bats once.   **B:** You did? Where were you?

C CATEGORIZE Talk about animals that people in the class have seen.
1. Make a list of the animals that pairs discussed in 5B.
2. Categorize the animals according to the descriptions in 1A.

■ I CAN TALK ABOUT WILDLIFE.

LESSON 3   DISCUSS ENDANGERED ANIMALS

LETI MOLINA
@LetiM

People are doing so many creative things to protect animals!

1 BEFORE YOU LISTEN

A How do humans put animals in danger? How do we help them?

B ▶01-15 VOCABULARY Listen. Then listen and repeat.

> **a deer**: a large wild animal that lives in forests and eats plants
> **soil**: the substance in which plants grow; dirt
> **a field**: an area of land where crops are grown
> **a crop**: a plant such as corn, wheat, or vegetables that farmers grow
> **an endangered species**: a type of animal or plant that soon might not exist anymore
> **a collar**: a narrow band put around the neck of an animal
> **a hook**: a curved piece of metal used for catching fish
> **a shelter**: a place to protect people or animals from bad weather or danger

C Write one of the words in 1B under each picture.

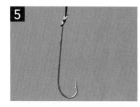

2 GRAMMAR *Though, although,* and *even though*

Use clauses beginning with *though, although,* and *even though* to show a contrast with the main idea. The main clause shows an unexpected result.

Though / although / even though clause	Main clause (an unexpected result)
Though hunting laws are great,	they aren't enough to protect all animals.
Although a butterfly is a tiny insect,	it can fly thousands of miles.
Even though it can be expensive,	protecting wildlife is important.

Though, although, and *even though* can also be used after the main clause, usually after a comma.

Main clause (an unexpected result)	*Though / although / even though* clause
Most spiders live for about a year,	**though** some live much longer.
Hippos can't swim,	**although** they spend most of the day in water.
Species will continue to disappear	**even though** we try to save them.

>> FOR PRACTICE, GO TO PAGE 127

3 LISTENING

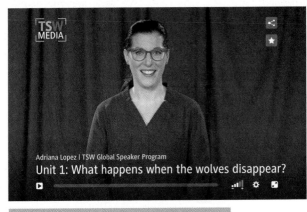

Adriana Lopez | TSW Global Speaker Program
Unit 1: What happens when the wolves disappear?

A ▶01-16 Listen or watch. What is the main idea?

Efforts to save endangered wildlife ___ .

a. have not been very successful
b. are important for both animals and humans
c. are getting more and more high-tech

B ▶01-17 Read the Listening Skill. Listen or watch again. How does the speaker answer each of these questions? Write a short answer.

1. Problem solved. But have you created a new problem? With no wolves around, deer invade the nearby hills. And the deer _____ .
2. Most countries have laws that limit hunting and fishing. Isn't that enough? _____ .
   Though hunting laws are great, _____ .

> **LISTENING SKILL** Listen for questions
>
> Speakers sometimes ask questions and then answer them. This is a way to highlight important ideas or transitions. Listen for questions to understand the important ideas in a talk.

C ▶01-18 Listen or watch again. Complete the chart.

Animal	Problem	Solution
	moving out of the jungle	tracking collars
	caught by mistake	magnetic fishhooks
monkeys		
turtles		turtle tunnels
bees	too many tall buildings.	

D VOCABULARY EXPANSION Read the sentences from the talk. What do the underlined expressions mean?

1. Every animal is part of <u>a complicated system</u>. If we allow whole species to disappear, no one can predict the result.
2. Although we can't predict the effects of allowing a specific animal to <u>die off</u>, we *do* know that our planet is stronger when there are many species of both animals and plants.
3. One way to save endangered animals is to <u>make sure</u> that people don't kill them. Most countries have laws that limit hunting and fishing.

E PAIRS Compare your answers in 3D.

4 DISCUSSION

A THINK Make a list of reasons why saving wildlife is important. Make a list of other things that money and effort could be spent on instead of helping animals.

B DISCUSS In small groups, talk about your ideas in 4A. Should the money and effort people are spending on animals be used in other ways? Why or why not?

Although it takes time and effort to save animals, it's worth it because …
Though I understand why people want to save wildlife, I think …

C EVALUATE As a class, discuss the reasons why people want to spend money and effort on saving wildlife or on something else instead. Vote on the three most convincing reasons for each argument.

☐ I CAN DISCUSS ENDANGERED ANIMALS.

LETI MOLINA

@LetiM

I read a great interview about a wildlife rescue center. Now I want to volunteer!

1 BEFORE YOU READ

A PAIRS Have you ever helped an animal? Talk about it.

Last year I found a baby bird that had fallen out of its nest ...

B ▶01-19 VOCABULARY Listen. Then listen and repeat. Do you know these words?

orphaned   fascinating   an enclosure   an environment   mimic   a natural habitat

⟩⟩ FOR DEFINITIONS AND PRACTICE, GO TO PAGE 127

2 READ

A PREVIEW Look at the title and the photographs. What do you think this text is about? Look at the format of the text. What does it tell you?

B ▶01-20 Read and listen to the interview. Were your answers correct?

A Place to Get Better

On the southern border of Costa Rica is a very special place where sick and injured wild animals are safe and cared for. It is the Jaguar Rescue Center. The center never turns away any wild animal brought to its door. I interviewed a volunteer, Kathleen, to find out more about this amazing place.

1 **So, Kathleen, tell me more about the center. What kinds of animals does it help?**

All kinds. Sloths, howler monkeys, porcupines, and more—any sick, injured, or orphaned animal. People in town, or sometimes the local police, see the animals in the road or while they're out hiking and bring them to the center.

2 **So what kinds of tasks do you do at the center?**

I do a lot of feeding and cleaning up. It's similar to having your own pets. We feed some of the baby animals with goat milk in bottles, and we help out in the kitchen to make food for the older animals.

a howler monkey

3 **Do you have a favorite kind of animal at the center?**

My favorite are the howler monkeys. They are so fascinating! Did you know that they are the loudest land animal? Their vocalizations can be heard clearly for five kilometers.

4 **Where do the howlers live in the center? I know that monkeys like to climb…**

a sloth

They eat and sleep in a very large enclosure, which we clean twice a day. The enclosure was created as an environment that closely mimics their natural habitat as much as possible, so there's plenty of space to climb, jump, swing, and play.

5 **Do the animals return to the jungle when they're healthy again?**

Yes! The goal is to return the animals to their natural habitat. Every afternoon, we take the healthy howlers into the jungle. If they don't come back, it means they are beginning a new life in the wild with a new family.

6 **It must be difficult to say good-bye to the howlers when they find their new home.**

Yes, but sometimes they come back to say hello. One of the howlers who had been successfully released back into the jungle returned one day with a surprise— a new baby! It's like she wanted to say "thank you" to the people who cared for her.

a porcupine

3 CHECK YOUR UNDERSTANDING

A Read the interview again. What is the interview mainly about? Circle the correct answer.

    a. what howler monkeys eat

    b. how a rescue center helps injured animals

    c. what to do if you find an injured animal

B Circle the correct answers, according to the interview.

1. Who finds the sick or injured animals and brings them to the center?

    a. the volunteers

    b. the police and hikers

    c. tourists

2. What does Kathleen say about the animals' diets?

    a. All the animals drink goat milk.

    b. Some of the food is prepared in the kitchen.

    c. The older animals find their own food.

3. What is one goal of the center?

    a. to release the animals back into the jungle

    b. to have the monkeys return to the center

    c. to watch how the animals behave in their natural habitats

C CLOSE READING Reread questions 5 and 6. Then answer the questions.

1. In question 5, what does *it means* refer to? _____

2. In question 6, what does *It's like* refer to? _____

D Read the Reading Skill. Match the main ideas below with the questions in the interview. Write *1–5*.

    ___ a. the howlers' habitat at the center

    ___ b. which animals are at the center

    ___ c. the goal of the center

    ___ d. the animal Kathleen likes best

    ___ e. what Kathleen does at the center

> **READING SKILL** Find the main idea
>
> The *main idea* is what a text is about. When you can find the main idea, it is easier to understand the text. When you read an interview, one way to find the main idea is to look at the questions.

E PAIRS What is the interview about? Retell the most important ideas. Use your own words.

The interview is about a volunteer and ...

> How else does the Jaguar Rescue Center help animals? 🔍

4 MAKE IT PERSONAL

A Think about ways to help sick, injured, or orphaned animals. Complete the chart with your ideas.

Things to do	Things to give to a rescue center	Names of rescue centers you know

B PAIRS Compare your ideas in 4A. Are either of you interested in helping animals?

We both plan to give money to a shelter ...

☐ I CAN READ ABOUT A WILDLIFE RESCUE CENTER.

LETI MOLINA
@LetiM

I finally posted photos from my trip to Panama last year! It was such an amazing experience!

1 BEFORE YOU WRITE

A What is the most beautiful place you have ever been to? What beautiful place do you want to visit?

B Read the travel blog. How does Leti feel when she thinks about Bocas del Toro? How do you know? Does the description make you want to visit Bocas del Toro?

Blog | About | Destinations | Contact

🔍 Search

BOCAS DEL TORO

Last year I went on vacation to Panama and stayed in the most beautiful place I've ever been—a place called Bocas del Toro. It's on the Caribbean Sea and has amazing beaches, trees, flowers, and wildlife—all in one place.

I loved walking on the beach and feeling the soft, white sand between my toes and the warm sun on my face. When I got a little too warm, I sat under a shady tree near the water and closed my eyes to hear the calming sound of the waves breaking on the shore. When I opened my eyes and looked around, I could see surfers riding on the blue-green waves, like dancers on top of the water. I could also see small, brown monkeys jumping and swinging through the many beautiful green trees. The sweet scent of the yellow and white ylang-ylang flowers mixed with the smell of the salty ocean. No perfume could smell any better! When I got hungry, I walked to a restaurant where they served delicious fresh fish and my favorite: sweet and salty fried plantains, which are similar to bananas.

Every time I think about my time in Panama, I can still see, smell, hear, feel, and taste that beautiful place, and for a few moments, I am back on that beach. I hope I can go back again soon!

Surfers riding waves

Ylang-ylang flowers

Fried plantains

2 FOCUS ON WRITING

Read the Writing Skill. Then reread the travel blog in 1B. Complete the chart with the things that the writer sees, feels, hears, smells, tastes.

WRITING SKILL Use sensory words

Writers use sensory words to help a reader make pictures of people, places, and things in their mind. Use sensory words that describe colors and sights, sounds, feelings, tastes, and smells—all the five senses—to make the reader "see" what you see.

See	Feel	Hear	Smell	Taste

3 PLAN YOUR WRITING

A Think about a beautiful place that you know. What do you see, feel, hear, smell, and taste when you think about this place? Take notes in the chart.

See	Feel	Hear	Smell	Taste

B PAIRS Describe the place that you chose using your notes from 3A. Try to picture the place that your partner describes.

I want to write about the Galapagos Islands in Ecuador. I saw many colorful birds and huge, slow-moving turtles ...

4 WRITE

Write a travel blog about a beautiful place that you know. Use sensory words to talk about what you saw, felt, heard, smelled, and tasted there. Try to "paint a picture" in the reader's mind. Use the blog in 1B as a model.

5 REVISE YOUR WRITING

A PAIRS Exchange and read each other's descriptions.
  1. Underline all of the sensory words.
  2. Did your partner use enough sensory words to help you make a picture in your mind?

B PAIRS Can you improve each other's descriptions? Make suggestions.

Revising tip

Wait a day before you revise your draft. This will help you see your writing with fresh eyes and make your writing better.

6 PROOFREAD

Read your description again. Check your
- spelling
- punctuation
- capitalization

■ I CAN WRITE A DESCRIPTION OF A PLACE.

PUT IT TOGETHER

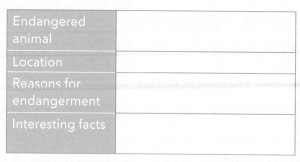

1 PRESENTATION PROJECT

A ▶01-21 Listen or watch. What is the topic of the presentation?

B ▶01-22 Listen or watch again. Complete the chart.

Endangered animal	
Location	
Reasons for endangerment	
Interesting facts	

C Read the Presentation Skill. Make a list of animals and size comparisons.

D Make your own presentation.

Step 1 Choose an endangered animal and find information about it. Complete a chart like the one in 1B.

Step 2 Prepare a two-minute presentation about your animal. Bring an item or picture related to your endangered animal. Remember to include comparisons for measurements.

Step 3 Give your presentation to the class. Answer questions and get feedback.

> **PRESENTATION SKILL**
>
> **Use comparisons for measurements**
> To make it easier for your audience to understand information about size, make comparisons to something the audience knows. For example, if you say that an animal is 15 meters (50 feet) long, you can also say that it is as long as a bus.

How did you do? Complete the self-evaluation on page 165.

2 REFLECT AND PLAN

A Look back through the unit. Check (✓) the things you learned. Highlight the things you need to learn.

Speaking objectives
- ☐ Talk about a weather event
- ☐ Talk about wildlife
- ☐ Discuss endangered animals

Vocabulary
- ☐ Weather
- ☐ Results of bad weather
- ☐ Animals
- ☐ Words to describe animals

Conversation
- ☐ Reply questions

Pronunciation
- ☐ Linking vowels with /w/ and /y/

Listening
- ☐ Listen for questions

Grammar
- ☐ *Get* to express change
- ☐ *So* and *such*
- ☐ *Though, although,* and *even though*

Reading
- ☐ Find the main idea

Writing
- ☐ Use sensory words

B What will you do to learn the things you highlighted? For example, use your app, review your Student Book, or do other practice. Make a plan.

In the app, do the Lesson 2 Vocabulary practice: Animals.

2 WHAT SKILLS ARE YOU LOOKING FOR?

LEARNING GOALS

In this unit, you
- ⊘ report what someone said
- ⊘ talk about job qualifications
- ⊘ discuss the future of work
- ⊘ read about job satisfaction
- ⊘ write about making a change

GET STARTED

A Read the unit title and learning goals.

B Look at the photo. What's going on?

C Now read Ed's message. Would you like to work in social media?

ED MILLER
@EdM

I've been doing some writing for the social media team. That's a field I'd love to get into!

ED MILLER
@EdM

I just heard some interesting news at work.

🔤 1 VOCABULARY Career advancement

A ▶02-01 **Listen. Then listen and repeat.**

> **an application:** a form that you complete to request a job or to join an organization
> **a candidate:** someone who wants to be chosen for a job
> **a job description:** a list of the responsibilities for a job
> **experience:** knowledge or skills that you have gotten by doing something
> **a job opening:** a job that is available
> **an entry-level job:** the lowest-level job in a company or department
> **a short-term position:** a temporary job
> **a permanent position:** a job that will continue
> **a promotion:** a move to a better position at work

B Complete the questions with words from 1A.

1. When was the last time you filled out a job _____ ?
2. How did you find out about the _____ ?
3. Was it a permanent position or a(n) _____ ?
4. Was it a high-level job or a(n) _____ ?
5. Have you ever gotten a(n) _____ at work?
6. Did you have the _____ for the job? Had you done similar work?

C PAIRS Ask and answer the questions in 1B.

2 GRAMMAR Reported speech

Reported speech uses reporting verbs like *say, mention,* and *tell.* Unlike direct speech, it does not quote the speaker's exact words: *He said that he wanted to be a chef.* When the reporting verb is in the past, we usually change the verb tense to show the correct time relationship.

	Direct speech: (She said,)	Reported speech
Present → Simple past	"I **want** to be a lawyer."	She said (that) she **wanted** to be a lawyer.
Past → Past perfect	"I **quit** my job yesterday."	She told me (that) she **had quit** her job the day before.
Present continuous → **Past continuous**	"I'm **applying** to law school."	She mentioned (that) she **was applying** to law school.
Present perfect → **Past perfect**	"I'**ve worked** here for three years."	She said (that) she **had worked** there for three years.
Will → Would	"I'**ll help** you with the project tomorrow."	She said (that) she **would help** me with the project the next day.
Can → Could	"I **can't finish** my work."	She said (that) she **couldn't finish** her work.

Note We use the present tense for general truths: *He said the sky is blue.*

>> FOR PRACTICE, GO TO PAGE 128

3 PRONUNCIATION

A ▶02-02 Read and listen to the pronunciation note.

B ▶02-03 Listen. Notice the stressed word in the examples. Then listen and repeat.

It's a **well**-known company.   The company is well **known**.

C ▶02-04 Listen. Circle the stressed words in the compound adjectives.

1. Many <u>part-time</u> jobs aren't <u>well paid</u>.
2. It's a <u>one-year</u> program at a <u>world-famous</u> school.
3. She's working <u>full time</u>, in an <u>entry-level</u> position.
4. He signed a <u>short-term</u>, <u>two-week</u> contract.

4 CONVERSATION

A ▶02-05 Listen or watch. What does Ed want?

a. to get a promotion
b. to join the social media team
c. to help with a new project

B ▶02-06 Listen or watch again. Answer the questions.

1. How did Pam get onto the social media team?
2. What is Ed's experience with the social media team?
3. What does Ed decide to do?

What do you think about Pam's decision to leave her job and go to law school? Is it a good idea? Why or why not?

C ▶02-07 FOCUS ON LANGUAGE Listen. Complete the conversation.

Leti: I talked to her a couple of months ago and she said _____ to law schools.

Ed: Law schools? Wow, that's a big change from working in social media.

Leti: Well, she said she _____ to be a lawyer.

5 TRY IT YOURSELF

A THINK Think about a job experience that someone told you about. Take notes in the chart.

Job description	How the person got the job	Did the person like the job?

B PAIRS Share the information in your chart. Report what the person said about his or her job.

My mother told me she'd had a short-term position as a server on a cruise ship ...

C REPORT Tell the class about the jobs you discussed. Who had the most unusual job experience? How many people said they liked their jobs?

■ I CAN REPORT WHAT SOMEONE SAID.

LESSON 2 — TALK ABOUT JOB QUALIFICATIONS

ED MILLER
@EdM

Time to talk to Mary about the social media job. I hope I don't look nervous!

1 VOCABULARY Describing employees

A ▶02-08 Read the infographic. Then listen and repeat the vocabulary words.

WHAT DO EMPLOYERS WANT? This is what they say.

A GREAT EMPLOYEE IS …

CREATIVE Employers are always looking for people with new ideas.

POSITIVE Every company wants people who have a good attitude.

RESPONSIBLE The best employees are ones an employer can trust. They show up on time and do their work carefully.

INDEPENDENT It's important for an employee to be able to work alone without someone always telling him or her what to do.

A GREAT EMPLOYEE HAS …

COMMUNICATION SKILLS Employers are looking for people who can speak, write, and express themselves.

LEADERSHIP SKILLS Good leaders don't just tell others what to do, they are also very good at working independently.

PROBLEM-SOLVING SKILLS Unexpected things happen in every job. Employers want to hire people who can think about and find solutions to problems.

TECHNICAL SKILLS Many jobs require people who can use specific technology, such as computer programs, machines, or tools.

B ▶02-09 Listen to the candidates for a design job. Circle the quality or skill they are describing.

1. She is *creative / positive*.
2. He is *responsible / independent*.
3. He has *leadership / problem-solving* skills.
4. She has *leadership / communication* skills.
5. She has *communication / technical* skills.
6. He is *positive / independent*.

C PAIRS Discuss jobs that require each quality in 1A. Explain your answers.

A: Chefs have to be creative. They always need to think of new dishes to cook.
B: True. And teachers also have to be creative. They need to think of new ways to teach lessons.

2 GRAMMAR Defining relative clauses

Defining relative clauses provide important information about a noun. They are placed directly after the noun they describe. These clauses begin with relative pronouns (*who*, *whom* and *that* for people, *that* and *which* for things).

	Noun	Subject relative pronoun	Subject relative clause
We want	someone	that who	has worked in social media.
I'm looking for	a job	that which	will use my leadership skills.

	Noun	Object relative pronoun	Object relative clause
We found	the person	(that) (whom)	we were looking for.
She has	a job	(that)	she loves.
Note: In object relative clauses, the relative pronoun is optional.			

>> FOR PRACTICE, GO TO PAGE 129

3 CONVERSATION SKILL

A ▶02-10 Read the conversation skill. Listen. Notice how the speakers ask if someone has time to talk.

1. Hey, Marlene. Got a second?
2. Excuse me, Paul. Can I talk to you for a minute?

B PAIRS Practice using different expressions to ask if your partner has time to talk.

A: Got a second?
B: Sure. What do you need?

A: Do you have a moment?
B: Of course. What can I do for you?

4 CONVERSATION

A ▶02-11 Listen or watch. How does Ed feel after talking to Mary?

a. He has less interest in the job.
b. He realizes he's not qualified for the job.
c. He feels encouraged to apply for the job.

B ▶02-12 Listen or watch again. Check (✓) your answers.

1. What qualities and skills does Mary say she is looking for?

☐ creative ☐ communication skills ☐ leadership skills
☐ independent ☐ problem-solving skills ☐ technical skills

2. What examples does Ed give of his social media experience?

☐ personal use ☐ a past job ☐ clubs in college

C ▶02-13 FOCUS ON LANGUAGE Listen. Complete the conversation.

> Do you think Ed is qualified for the job? Why or why not?

Ed: So, what kind of candidate are you looking for?

Mary: Well, let's see. The person _____ is creative. We want to hear a lot of good, new ideas.

Ed: Of course.

Mary: And obviously we want someone _____ .

5 TRY IT YOURSELF

RESTAURANT MANAGER	NURSE	GAME TESTER
Manage busy family restaurant with 25 employees. Full time.	Nurse in large hospital. Night shift. Good salary and benefits.	Help team with testing of new video games. Part time.

A THINK Read the ads.
What qualities do you think are needed for each job?

Restaurant Manager	Nurse	Game Tester

B PAIRS Discuss your ideas. Would you be interested in one of these positions? Do you know someone who would be interested?

My cousin would be perfect for the restaurant manager job. He's been managing my uncle's restaurant part time for a couple of years. He has great leadership skills.

☐ **I CAN TALK ABOUT JOB QUALIFICATIONS.**

ED MILLER
@EdM

Ever wonder what our jobs will be like 25 years from now?

1 BEFORE YOU LISTEN

A In your country, what jobs have been disappearing in the last 25 years? What new jobs have been created or become more common?

B ▶02-14 VOCABULARY Listen. Then listen and repeat.

> **a bank teller:** a cashier who deals with customers at a bank
> **automation:** the use of machines, not people, to do a job
> **a programmer:** someone who writes programs for computers
> **a technician:** someone whose job involves using special equipment or machines to do something
> **an engineer:** someone whose job is to design and build machines, roads, and bridges
> **an accountant:** someone whose job is to keep records of how much money a business or person has received and spent
> **a landscaper:** someone whose job is to arrange where plants will grow
> **an industry:** all of the businesses that make or do a particular type of thing
> **manufacturing:** the business of using machines to make things

C Complete the sentences with words from 1B.
1. My brother is a(n) _____ . He designs car engines. He's worked in the automotive _____ for 15 years and says things are really changing.
2. The _____ at ABC Corp got fired for making a huge mistake with the taxes.
3. There are some job listings for the new hospital. They're looking for an X-ray _____ , and they are also going to hire a(n) _____ to redesign the gardens.
4. There used to be a lot of _____ in this town, but all of the factories have shut down.
5. I heard they're hiring a(n) _____ to fix the software so it will work better for our needs.
6. Miranda used to be a(n) _____ , but she got tired of standing at a counter all day.
7. There used to be 200 workers at this factory, but because of _____ , there are 50 now.

D PAIRS Tell your partner about someone you know who has or wants one of the jobs in 1B. Share what you know about the person's qualities or interests.

My friend Ana is studying to be an engineer. I think she wants to work on planes.

2 GRAMMAR *So and therefore*

Use *so* and *therefore* to make conclusions.		
The ATM made running a bank cheaper,	**so**	banks opened more branches.
Appliances and phones are cheaper,	**so**	people replace those things more often.
The new jobs require a lot of education.	**Therefore,**	we'll see more work for teachers.
Automation has made goods cheaper;	**therefore,**	people have more money to spend.

Notes
- Use a comma before *so* and after *therefore*.
- You can use a semicolon to join sentences with *therefore*. *The new jobs require a lot of education;* **therefore,** *we'll see more jobs for teachers.*

>> FOR PRACTICE, GO TO PAGE 130

3 LISTENING

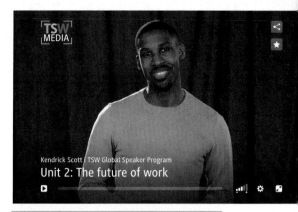

Kendrick Scott | TSW Global Speaker Program
Unit 2: The future of work

A ▶02-15 Listen or watch. What is the main idea?

   a. In the future, many people will lose their jobs to automation.

   b. Automation can create jobs and improve lives.

   c. Automation has created many jobs in the past.

B ▶02-16 Read the Listening Skill. Listen or watch again. Complete each counter-argument using information from the video.

1. Automation has destroyed jobs, but

   _____ .

2. Many of the tasks they once did can now be done by machines and intelligent software. However, all of this automation

   _____ .

3. Technology may have changed the way we work, but

   _____ .

> **LISTENING SKILL**
> **Listen for counter-arguments**
>
> Speakers sometimes bring up ideas that they disagree with to help make their point. They may follow these ideas with *but*, *however*, or *on the other hand* to introduce their own contrasting idea.

C ▶02-17 Listen or watch again. Circle the correct answer.

1. According to the speaker, what will automation create?

   a. jobs for educated people   b. many different kinds of jobs

2. What positive effect of automation on manufacturing does the speaker discuss?

   a. cheaper goods   b. more interesting work

3. Why does the speaker have such a positive view of the future?

   a. because educational levels are improving along with technology

   b. because automation has created new jobs in the past

D VOCABULARY EXPANSION Read the sentences from the talk. What do the underlined expressions mean?

1. Self-driving vehicles are on their way to <u>eliminating</u> millions of driving jobs.

2. Automation in factories has made <u>essential</u> goods cheaper, so more people can buy the things they need.

3. I have no doubt that technology will <u>lead to</u> other new jobs that we can't even imagine yet.

E PAIRS Compare your answers in 3D.

4 DISCUSSION

A THINK What effects do you think automation will have on employment? Choose an industry, for example, food service, health care, entertainment, transportation, or manufacturing. Make a list of positive and negative effects that technology might have on that industry.

B DISCUSS In small groups, share your ideas in 4A.

More people will start using apps to order food, so restaurants will need fewer servers.

C EVALUATE As a class, discuss the effects of automation on each of the chosen industries. For which ones does the class predict the most negative or positive effects? What can be done to lessen the negative effects?

■ I CAN DISCUSS THE FUTURE OF WORK.

ED MILLER
@EdM

How many of us actually get to work at our dream job?

1 BEFORE YOU READ

A PAIRS Is it more important to have a job you love or a job that pays you well? Explain your answer.

B ▶02-18 VOCABULARY Listen. Then listen and repeat. Do you know these words?

a passion	a salary	satisfaction	clergy	a psychologist
a connection	a dead end	take pride in	spare time	donate

>> FOR DEFINITIONS AND PRACTICE, GO TO PAGE 130

2 READ

A PREVIEW Look at the title and the photograph. What advice do you think the article will give?

B ▶02-19 Read and listen to the article. Was your prediction correct?

HAPPY WORK, HAPPY LIFE

People talk a lot about finding their "dream job" or "following their passion." But what if your dream job is just that—a dream? The fact is, most of us take, and keep, jobs for practical reasons like
5 location or salary. But no one wants to spend the majority of their waking hours doing something that they don't enjoy. What if you could find happiness and meaning in any job—even when it isn't the one you dreamed of?

10 First, what exactly makes a job meaningful? A study by the University of Chicago found that a feeling of purpose, and particularly the ability to help others, can lead to higher job satisfaction. According to the study, those who report feeling
15 the most satisfied in their careers include clergy, firefighters, teachers, and psychologists. These are all careers that involve helping people in some way.

What if helping people isn't a key feature of your job? Maybe you need to look at it differently. A
20 great way to find meaning at work is through connection with co-workers, customers, or clients. For example, Luke was a custodian at a hospital, a job many people would think is a dead end. Luke's job duties included things like cleaning
25 rooms but not working with people. However, Luke told researchers that through his job, he was making patients feel more comfortable, and he took pride in being able to help people who were sick.

30 It's also important to remember your job can be what allows you to do other important things in your life. Maybe the schedule allows you to volunteer in your community in your spare time, or maybe getting a steady paycheck means
35 you're able to donate to good causes that you care about. You can find meaning in your job in more indirect ways like these.

Studies also show that finding job satisfaction through helping others contributes to
40 happiness in your life in general. According to psychologist Shawn Anchor, "If you can raise somebody's level of positivity in the present, then their brain experiences what we now call a happiness advantage….Your intelligence rises,
45 your creativity rises, your energy levels rise." This can lead to more success and happiness in your job and in your life.

3 CHECK YOUR UNDERSTANDING

A Read the article again. What does the article say is the key to being happy at work?

a. a high salary   b. friendly co-workers   c. helping others

B Answer the questions with information from the article.

1. What does the writer say about finding satisfaction in your job?

   _____

2. Even if your job isn't your dream job, what is important to find?

   _____

3. With a steady paycheck, what can you do?

   _____

C CLOSE READING Reread lines 10–17 in the article. Think about the words *others*, *those*, and *these*. Circle the correct answers.

1. What does *others* refer to?
   a. people that you can connect with at work
   b. people who are satisfied with their jobs
   c. people who work as clergy, psychologists, etc.
2. What does *those* refer to?
   a. people who need help
   b. people who report feeling fulfilled in their careers
   c. satisfying jobs
3. What does *these* refer to?
   a. clergy, firefighters, teachers, and psychologists
   b. people that you can connect with at work
   c. people who report feeling fulfilled in their careers

D Read the Reading Skill. Then underline the rhetorical questions in the article. What were your own ideas after you read each question?

E PAIRS What is the article about? Summarize the most important ideas. Use your own words.

The article is about what makes a job meaningful and …

> **READING SKILL**
> **Understand rhetorical questions**
>
> Writers often ask questions without expecting an answer. This gives readers an opportunity to actively think about the topic and form their own ideas before they read what the writer has to say.

What other advice do experts give for being happy with your job?

4 MAKE IT PERSONAL

A For you, what are the most important things about a job? Money? Location? Salary? Helping others? Put your ideas in order from most to least important.

Most important	
↓	
Least important	

B PAIRS Compare your ideas in 4A. Give reasons for your opinions. Explain your reasons. What jobs do you think would be best for you?

The location of a job is important to me. I don't want to travel a long way to work.

■ I CAN READ ABOUT JOB SATISFACTION.

ED MILLER
@EdM

Making a career move is
hard to do.

1 BEFORE YOU WRITE

A Have you or someone you know ever changed
jobs or made another life change? What good advice have you heard about doing this?

B Read the article about changing careers. What two question words does the writer use to
organize the advice? Do you think she gives good advice?

CHANGING CAREERS: THE WHY AND THE WHAT

Janet Garcia, Staff Writer at Life Coaching Magazine

Changing careers can be exciting, but it can also be frightening because you are trying
something new. Don't worry! Before filling out applications, ask yourself these important
questions to find your path to a new, fulfilling career.

First, ask yourself: *Why do I want to change my career?* This is a very important question to
answer in order to find a job that you will be happy in. For example, are you now in an office all
day but you love to be outside? Do you work in a small company but would prefer to be in a big one so that you
have more opportunities for promotions? The answers to this question will give you important information for taking
your next steps and help you focus your search in the right area.

Now that you have figured out the *why*, you have to think about the *what*. Ask yourself what careers could give
you what you need. There are many ways to find information on possible careers. Of course, the internet is full
of information. Just do a search with key words from your *why* questions. For example, "outdoors, environment,
careers" will give you lots of ideas about environmental jobs where you can spend time outside.

Another way to get ideas is to ask your friends and family what careers they think would be best for you. Since they
know you the best, they have a good understanding of your strengths, weaknesses, and what makes you happy.
Keep an open mind, and you might hear some interesting suggestions that you hadn't thought of! Look for my next
post, where I'll talk about the *how* and the *when* of finding your perfect career.

C Reread the article. Fill in the chart. Write advice from the article in the middle circles. Write
the reasons for the advice in the outer circles.

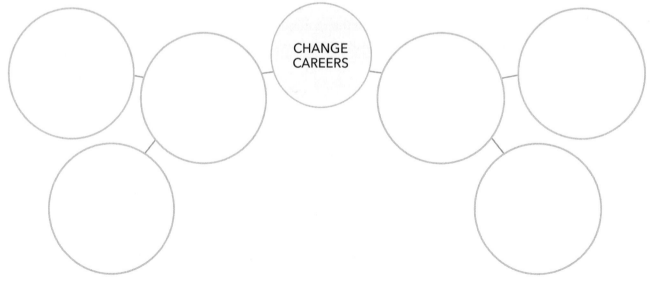

CHANGE
CAREERS

2 FOCUS ON WRITING

Read the Writing Skill. Then circle the linking expressions and underline the reasons in the article in 1B.

> **WRITING SKILL** Use linking expressions
>
> Good writers use linking expressions to show the reason something happens or the purpose of an action. Some linking expressions are *because, due to, in order to, so that*, and *since*. Sometimes the reason comes before the linking word and sometimes after.

3 PLAN YOUR WRITING

A Think about advice you can give someone who wants to make a change in his or her life, such as moving to another city, changing schools, or getting a new job. Take notes in the chart.

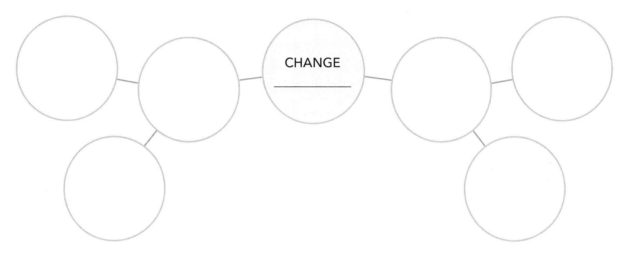

CHANGE

B PAIRS Talk about your ideas. Suggest ways your partner can improve or add to his or her ideas.

I want to write about changing to another school. One good piece of advice I heard was ...

4 WRITE

Write an article about making a life change. Describe the specific type of change and then give your advice. Write at least two pieces of advice. Remember to use linking expressions to show reason and purpose. Use the article in 1B as a model.

Writing tip

When you're writing an informal article, imagine you're talking to a friend. This will help to make your writing more relaxed and natural.

5 REVISE YOUR WRITING

A PAIRS Exchange articles and read your partner's advice about make a life change.

1. Circle the life change. Underline the linking expressions.
2. Did your partner give at least two pieces of advice?
3. Did your partner give information to show the purpose of the advice?

B PAIRS Can your partner improve his or her article? Make suggestions.

6 PROOFREAD

Read your article again. Check your

- spelling
- punctuation
- capitalization

■ I CAN WRITE ABOUT MAKING A CHANGE.

PUT IT TOGETHER

1 PRESENTATION PROJECT

A ▶02-20 Listen or watch. What is the topic of the presentation?

B ▶02-21 Listen or watch again. Answer the questions.

1. What job was Junio interested in? _____
2. Why was he interested in it?
   _____
3. How was it related to qualities and interests he had?
   _____
4. How did he first learn about the job?
   _____

C Read the Presentation Skill. How can watching or listening to recordings of yourself help you improve your presentation? Make a list of ideas.

D Make your own presentation.

Step 1 Think about a job you were interested in when you were a child.

- What job were you interested in?
- Why were you interested in it?
- How was it related to qualities and interests you had?
- How did you find out about the job?
- Are you still interested in it?

Step 2 Prepare a two-minute presentation about the job you were interested in. Bring an item or picture that is related to that job.

Step 3 Give your presentation to the class. Answer questions and get feedback.

> **PRESENTATION SKILL**
>
> **Practice by listening to recordings of yourself**
> Record yourself to prepare for presentations. Listen for parts where you can make your ideas and pronunciation clearer.

How did you do? Complete the self-evaluation on page 165.

2 REFLECT AND PLAN

A Look back through the unit. Check (✓) the things you learned. Highlight the things you need to learn.

Speaking objectives
- ☐ Report what someone said
- ☐ Talk about job qualifications
- ☐ Discuss the future of work

Vocabulary
- ☐ Career advancement
- ☐ Describing employees

Conversation
- ☐ Ask if someone has time to talk

Pronunciation
- ☐ Stress in compound adjectives

Listening
- ☐ Listen for counter-arguments

Grammar
- ☐ Reported speech
- ☐ Defining relative clauses
- ☐ *So* and *therefore*

Reading
- ☐ Understand rhetorical questions

Writing
- ☐ Use linking expressions

B What will you do to learn the things you highlighted? For example, use your app, review your Student Book, or do other practice. Make a plan.

‹ Notes   Done

Review the grammar chart in Lesson 2, page 20.

_____
_____
_____

3 WHAT'S GOING ON?

GET STARTED

A Read the unit title and learning goals.

B Look at the photo. What's going on?

C Now read Paula's message. What do you do for fun when you travel to a big city?

PAULA FLOREZ

@PaulaF

I'm in New York for the next week. Lots of work to do, but hopefully I can find time for some fun!

PAULA FLOREZ
@PaulaF

There's so much to do in New York!

 1 VOCABULARY Cultural events

A ▶03-01 **Listen. Then listen and repeat.**

a concert

a magic show

a puppet show

a food fair

an art exhibit

fireworks

a baking contest

a carnival

a parade

a race

B ▶03-02 **Listen and circle the correct event.**

1. a. a race   b. an art exhibit   c. fireworks
2. a. a magic show   b. a baking contest   c. a carnival
3. a. a food fair   b. a concert   c. a magic show
4. a. an art exhibit   b. a concert   c. fireworks
5. a. a food fair   b. a magic show   c. a carnival
6. a. a baking contest b. a race   c. fireworks
7. a. a concert   b. a carnival   c. a food fair
8. a. fireworks   b. an art exhibit   c. a magic show

C PAIRS **Which of the events in 1A have you attended or seen on TV or the internet? Discuss your experiences.**

A: I've never been to a baking contest, but I've seen one on TV.
B: I haven't been to one either, but my cousin was in a bread-baking contest once. She makes really good bread!

2 GRAMMAR Superlative adjectives

Use *one of, some of,* or *among* with superlative adjectives. We usually omit the noun after the superlative if it is the same as the subject.

Superlative adjectives
1 syllable: *new → the newest*
2+ syllables: *exciting → the most exciting*
Ending in *y: pretty → the prettiest*

Subject + verb	One of / some of / among	Superlative adjective	Plural / non-count noun	
Calypso is	**one of**	the best	restaurants	in New York.
The band played	**some of**	the most beautiful	music	I've ever heard.
He is	**among**	the greatest	performers	of all time.
That meal was	**one of**	the most delicious	(meals)	I've ever eaten.
This restaurant is	**one of**	the busiest	(restaurants)	in the city.

>> FOR PRACTICE, GO TO PAGE 131

3 PRONUNCIATION

A ▶03-03 Read and listen to the pronunciation note.

B ▶03-04 Listen. Notice how *of* is pronounced in the examples. Then listen and repeat.

one of the best restaurants   a few of our friends

C ▶03-05 Listen. Cross out the letter *f* in *of* when *of* is pronounced /ə/. Then listen and repeat.

1. some of my friends
2. one of each type
3. one of the best concerts
4. some of the best food
5. most of an hour
6. one of the funniest movies

4 CONVERSATION

A ▶03-06 Listen or watch. Where are Ed and Paula going to go?

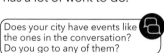

B ▶03-07 Listen or watch again. Circle the correct answer.

1. Where is Ed going tonight?
   a. a David Bowie concert   b. the City-Wide festival
   c. a carnival
2. Which three things are happening this weekend?
   a. concert, carnival, food fair   b. parade, concert, race
   c. carnival, parade, food fair
3. Why is Paula unsure about going with Ed?
   a. She doesn't like the band.   b. She's going to Mexico.   c. She has a lot of work to do.

C ▶03-08 FOCUS ON LANGUAGE Listen. Complete the conversation.

Does your city have events like the ones in the conversation? Do you go to any of them?

Paula:	Calypso is supposed to be _____ in New York!
Ed:	Is it? I've never eaten there.
Paula:	Yeah. I haven't been to that many restaurants here, but I ate there last time I was in town. I've wanted to go back ever since. It was _____ I've ever had.

5 TRY IT YOURSELF

A THINK Think about one of the best events or performances you have attended. Make notes about what made it so memorable.

Where	What	Memorable because ...

B PAIRS Talk about the event or performance.

A: One of the best events I've ever attended was the city carnival last year.
B: Why was it so good?
A: Because I went with my three best friends, and we had so much fun.

C REPORT Tell the class about the events you discussed. Which was the most popular?

☐ I CAN TALK ABOUT CULTURAL EVENTS.

LESSON 2 GIVE OPINIONS ABOUT TV SHOWS

PAULA FLOREZ
@PaulaF

Two months until the new season of *Circle of Kings*. What should I watch until then?

1 VOCABULARY Describing TV shows

A Read the chart. How does your TV-watching time compare to the average for your region?

B ▶03-09 Listen. Then listen and repeat.

> **an episode:** a TV show that is one in a series
> **a season:** a series of TV episodes shown during a certain time period
> **a season finale:** the last episode in a season
> **a cast:** all of the actors in a TV show
> **a trailer:** a short advertisement for a movie or TV show
> **a plot:** the events that form the main story of a TV show, movie, or book
> **a main character:** one of the most important people in a story
> **a minor character:** a person with a small role in a story
> **a spoiler:** information about a TV show that can ruin a surprise for the first-time viewer

Average Time Spent Watching TV
(including TV sets, computers, phones, and tablets)

Region	Minutes per day
Asia Pacific	154.5
Central and Eastern Europe	222.9
Latin America	199.0
North America	292.6
Middle East and North Africa	249.7
Western Europe	220.5
Rest of World	211.0

C Complete the ad. Use words from 1B.

JJ IS BACK!

Julia Jones, (1) _____ Five begins next weekend! We'll finally find out whether Julia survived falling off the mountain in last year's (2) _____ . There are only seven (3) _____ this time—one each Thursday for the next seven weeks. A new actor has been added to the fantastic (4) _____ , but we're not going to tell you who! Click this link to watch the (5) _____ now. But don't worry—there are no (6) _____ !

D PAIRS Discuss the TV show in the ad in 1C. Use your imagination. What do you think will happen in the first episode and the season finale?

A: Well, Julia's the main character, so we'll find out she's alive in the first episode.
B: Yeah. Maybe we'll see her climbing back up the mountain.

2 GRAMMAR Negative questions

Use negative questions with *be* and *do* to find out if someone agrees with your opinion.

Negative *be*		Negative *do*	
Isn't	it a great show?	Don't	you love Princess Kaliya?
Aren't	spoilers annoying?	Don't	you think it's a great show?
Wasn't	that season finale exciting?	Didn't	you love her little smile?
Weren't	you happy with the ending?	Didn't	you enjoy the plot?

>> FOR PRACTICE, GO TO PAGE 132

3 CONVERSATION SKILL

A ▶03-10 Read the conversation skill. Listen. Notice how the speakers disagree.

1. A: Wasn't that a terrible episode?
   B: Actually, I thought it was pretty good.
2. A: Don't you love Jon Bolo? He's such a great actor.
   B: I don't know. I think he's kind of boring.

> **Disagree with an opinion**
>
> When we disagree with someone's opinions, we often use language that softens our answers.
> *Actually*, I didn't like it that much.
> *Not really*. I was a little bored.
> *I guess* it was OK, but it wasn't great.
> *I don't know*. It was *kind of* boring.

B Complete the questions with your own ideas. Then ask a partner, and practice disagreeing.

1. Wasn't  great?
2. Don't you love 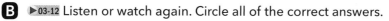 ?

4 CONVERSATION

A ▶03-11 Listen or watch. What are they talking about?

a. a show they both like
b. a show that Paula hasn't seen
c. a show that Ed doesn't like

B ▶03-12 Listen or watch again. Circle all of the correct answers.

1. Why do they think the third season of *Circle of Kings* isn't as good as previous seasons?
   a. The season finale was boring.
   b. The writing isn't as good anymore.
   c. The main character isn't interesting.
   d. There are too many minor characters.
2. What do they say about Princess Kaliya?
   a. She was in a fight in a forest.
   b. She looks angry all the time.
   c. She died in the last season.
   d. She appears in the trailer.

C ▶03-13 FOCUS ON LANGUAGE Listen. Complete the conversation.

Paula: _____ ?

Ed: It was! And now I'm dying for Season 4 to come out. I need to know if Alan Storm is going to live!

Paula: I know … though honestly, he's one of my least favorite characters. _____ the actor is kind of annoying?

Ed: Actually, I like him.

> Ed binge-watched the third season, meaning he watched a lot of episodes in one sitting. Do you think this is a good way to watch TV? Why or why not?

5 TRY IT YOURSELF

A THINK Make a list of TV shows you like now or liked in the past.

B PAIRS Talk about your lists. Try to find two or three shows on which you agree.

A: Have you seen Circle of Kings?
B: Oh yeah. Wasn't it great?
A: Actually, I didn't like it that much. How about Doctor Madison?
B: Oh, I love that show!

C COMPARE Tell the class about your findings. Is there any show that most students like?

■ I CAN GIVE OPINIONS ABOUT TV SHOWS.

LESSON 3 DISCUSS WAYS TO MAKE LIFE MORE INTERESTING

PAULA FLOREZ
@PaulaF

Ever feel like you're always doing the same old thing? What if you had an app that planned your life for you?

1 BEFORE YOU LISTEN

A How often do you meet new people, eat at new restaurants, or visit new places? Would you like to do these things more often?

B ▶03-14 VOCABULARY Listen. Then listen and repeat.

> **satisfied:** feeling that something is good
> **an app (an application):** a piece of computer software that does a particular job
> **random:** happening or chosen without any plan or pattern
> **a destination:** the place you are traveling to
> **a networking event:** a meeting for people who do the same kind of work, for information and support
> **a rally:** a large public meeting held in support of something

C PAIRS Discuss the questions and statements.

1. Describe a time you felt satisfied.
2. If you could travel anywhere, what would your destination be?
3. Do you know about any networking events? What do people do there?
4. Describe a rally you went to, heard about, or saw on TV.
5. What is one event you never want to miss out on?
6. What apps do you use the most?
7. When you listen to music, do you prefer to listen to songs at random or to make a playlist?

A: If I could travel anywhere, my destination would be Patagonia. I've heard it's beautiful!
B: That sounds interesting. What would you like to do there?

2 GRAMMAR Adverbial intensifiers with adjectives

Use adverbs such as *amazingly*, *extremely*, and *incredibly* to emphasize adjectives.

	Adverb	Adjective	
He had an	**extremely**	nice	life.
Some of the events were	**incredibly**	interesting	to attend.
It is	**surprisingly**	easy	to get stuck.
It was	**unusually**	warm	last September.
Note: *Very* and *really* are also intensifiers.			

>> FOR PRACTICE, GO TO PAGE 133

3 LISTENING

David Cruz | TSW Global Speaker Program
Unit 3: The random life

A ▶03-15 Listen or watch. What was the purpose of Max's apps?

B ▶03-16 Read the Listening Skill. Listen or watch again. Complete the lists of examples.

1. Max went to random public events. **Examples:** a _____ class, a _____ event, a _____ at someone's house.
2. He let the app choose locations around the world. **Examples:** _____ , _____ , _____ , the United Arab Emirates, Slovenia.
3. He used apps to decide how to spend his time. **Examples:** which _____ to attend, which _____ to eat at, and which _____ to visit.

LISTENING SKILL
Listen for lists of examples

Speakers sometimes use lists of examples to illustrate their main ideas. The examples help you get a clearer picture of what the speaker means.

C ▶03-17 Listen or watch again. Circle the correct answer.

1. Why wasn't Max satisfied with his old life?
   a. His job wasn't very interesting.
   b. He felt like he wasn't having many new experiences.
   c. He didn't find his friends very interesting.
2. How did people react to Max when he showed up at their events?
   a. They often told him that the events were private.
   b. They wanted to know who invited him to the party.
   c. They were friendly and interested in him.
3. In the end, how did he feel about letting the apps make decisions for him?
   a. It helped him see the world in a new way.
   b. It was valuable, but too expensive.
   c. It didn't change his life in any important ways.

D VOCABULARY EXPANSION Read the sentences. What do the underlined expressions mean?

1. He felt like he was always doing the same things, hanging out with the same people, and missing out on interesting experiences. He felt like he was living in a bubble.
2. Some of the events weren't that exciting, but some of them were incredibly interesting. And all of them were things he wouldn't have thought to try on his own.
3. He found that letting the apps make his choices for him opened his mind to new experiences. Really, it gave him a whole new understanding of the world.

E PAIRS Compare your answers in 3D.

4 DISCUSSION

A THINK Would you let an app tell you what to do? What problems do you see with this?

B DISCUSS In small groups, share your ideas from 4A. Make a list of other ways that people can break out of their "bubbles."

Max's apps probably sent him to some extremely boring events, and I don't have time for that. I'd rather ask my friends for ideas.

C EVALUATE As a class, discuss the ideas in 4B. Decide which ones are the best.

☐ I CAN DISCUSS WAYS TO MAKE MORE LIFE INTERESTING.

PAULA FLOREZ
@PaulaF

Imagine a TV show that only showed the view from a train window. Would you watch it?

1 BEFORE YOU READ

A PAIRS What kinds of TV shows do you enjoy watching: reality shows, crime shows, comedies? How do your favorite shows make you feel?

I love watching comedies. They make me feel relaxed and happy.

B ▶03-18 VOCABULARY Listen. Then listen and repeat. Do you know these words?

a recommendation	stressful	take (something) by storm	an anniversary
uneventful	a producer	a break	a viewer

>> FOR DEFINITIONS AND PRACTICE, GO TO PAGE 133

2 READ

A PREVIEW Look at the title and the photographs. What do you think this article is about?

B ▶03-19 Read and listen to the article. Was your prediction correct?

Take It Slow

Many of us watch TV to relax, but have you ever noticed how stressful watching TV can be? Many reality TV shows make you nervous because you don't know if your favorite performer will make it to the next round. Sports are thrilling,
5 but you get incredibly anxious if your team is losing. Don't you get tired of all the stress and just want to relax? If so, I have the perfect recommendation for you: Slow TV!

The first Slow TV show took Norway by storm in 2009. It started because of the 100th anniversary of the Bergen
10 Railway. To celebrate, some TV producers decided to attach a camera to the front of a train and broadcast its seven-hour journey through Norway, from Bergen to Oslo. What happens on the train? Murder? Romance? No—nothing happens—just the beautiful Norwegian scenery going by.
15 And Norwegians loved it! In a country of 5 million people, 1.2 million watched this uneventful train ride.

And that was just the beginning. In 2011, Norwegian TV producers showed a cruise ship traveling from the southern end of Norway to the northern end. The whole show was
20 five days—that's 134 hours and 42 minutes of TV. This time over 3 million people watched—even the queen! Since then, more Slow TV programs have been made—eight hours of sweater knitting, 18 hours of salmon fishing, and 168 hours of reindeer traveling across Lapland.

25 Why do so many people want to watch Slow TV? After all, nothing happens. According to Thomas Hellum, one of the producers of Slow TV, "The journey is in real time and people feel like they are there." He says that viewers feel like they are experiencing it with other people. At the same time,
30 people have their own feelings and memories and make their own stories about what is happening. In Slow TV, no producer is making decisions about how to "tell a story" because there is no story!

Of course, no one watches five days and nights of TV. So
35 what do viewers do? Some use it to relax for a little while—to take a break from a busy day. Others multitask. They have the TV on while they do housework or study.
Slow TV gives us something other TV programs can't. You don't have to think about the past or worry about the
40 future—you can just be in the present. You can even take a nap—you're not going to miss anything!

3 CHECK YOUR UNDERSTANDING

A Read the article again. According to the article, why do people like Slow TV? Circle the correct answer.

   a. It's relaxing.   b. It tells a good story.   c. They can watch it anywhere.

B Circle the correct answers, according to the article.

1. The first Slow TV show showed ___ .
   a. the queen of Norway
   b. a story about the Bergen Railway
   c. the Norwegian countryside
2. According to Thomas Hellum, people enjoy Slow TV because they ___ .
   a. like trains and boats
   b. can multitask while it's on
   c. can make up their own stories about what is happening
3. Many people ___ while they watch Slow TV.
   a. get excited
   b. do other things
   c. talk about the show with their friends

C CLOSE READING Reread lines 35-37. Think about the words *some*, *they*, and *others*. Then choose the correct answers.

1. What do the words *some*, *they*, and *others* refer to?
   a. TV shows   b. devices   c. viewers
2. Why does the author use different words to refer to the same thing?
   a. because good writing uses a variety of words
   b. because it is good to make the reader think about different details
   c. because readers need a good memory to read an article

D Read the Reading Skill. Go back to the article and underline the words that help you construct a clear mental image. For you, which part of the text was the easiest to "see"?

> **READING SKILL Construct mental images**
>
> Writers often use descriptive language to help readers picture, or "see," what they are writing about. Good descriptive writing uses adjectives (*beautiful, exciting, happy*) and adverbs (*fast, suddenly, hard*). This helps readers form a mental image and also makes the reading experience more interesting.

E PAIRS What is the article about? Summarize the most important ideas. Use your own words.

The article is about an unusual type of TV show ...

> What other Slow TV shows are available to watch? 🔍

4 MAKE IT PERSONAL

A Think of other ideas for Slow TV shows. Complete the chart with your ideas.

Subject	Description	Number of hours

B PAIRS Compare your ideas in 4A. Explain.

I think it's a good subject for Slow TV because ...

▢ I CAN READ A TV REVIEW.

LESSON 5   WRITE ABOUT LOCAL EVENTS

PAULA FLOREZ
@PaulaF

There's so much going on this weekend and not enough time to do it all! How do I decide?

1 BEFORE YOU WRITE

A How do you find out about events where you live? Do you ask friends? Do you look at any online guides or websites?

B Read the subtitles and the event guide. Match the subtitles to the correct sections.

| Eat   See an Exhibit   Go to a Show |

Home | News | Sport | Business   Search

AROUND TOWN   Looking for something to do this weekend? Here are some ideas:

_____
○ Check out the Johnson History Museum's new dinosaurs. Children will be fascinated by the new full-size T. Rex skeleton. There are also recordings of what scientists think some dinosaurs sounded like. It'll be music to your ears!

○ The Modern Gallery has some amazing nature photographs on display. "Hiding in Plain Sight: Animal Camouflage" shows you insects that look like leaves, frogs that look like rocks, owls that look like part of a tree. See how animals use their environment to hide from dangerous predators.

_____
○ Summer is here, and so is the Longman Park Concert Series. First up on Friday night is the popular local band, The Giant Cats. Sit under the stars, sing along to your favorite songs, and if you get hungry during the show, stop by the food trucks to get something delicious to eat.

○ At the Laugh Factory, see Bobby Felder, the star of TV's *Bobby's House*. His stand-up comedy is hilarious and will have you laughing from start to finish.

_____
○ The Farmer's Market opens on Saturday. You can stock up on fresh fruits and vegetables and try delicious baked items.

○ Do you watch the TV show *Kitchen Wars*? If so, you'll want to come to the Foodie Festival at Center Park on Sunday from 12:00 to 3:00, when all the contestants will be cooking up their amazing dishes.

○ The International Food Fair will take place in the Chen Auditorium at State College. Try foods from around the world and watch interesting cooking demonstrations so you can make the dishes at home!

C Read the event guide again. Complete the chart.

Category	Eat		
Events			
Things to do at events			

2 FOCUS ON WRITING

Read the Writing Skill. Circle the categories in the event guide. Then underline the words in each section that are related to the category.

3 PLAN YOUR WRITING

A What kinds of things can you do in your city? What categories can you think of? Complete the chart with your categories and event information.

Category			
Events			
Things to do at events			

B PAIRS Talk about your ideas. Suggest ways your partner can improve or add to his or her ideas.

My city has a lot of festivals so that can be one category ...

4 WRITE

Write an event guide for things to do in your city. Use at least three categories to organize the events that you choose. Use the event guide in 1B as a model.

5 REVISE YOUR WRITING

A PAIRS Exchange event guides and read your partner's ideas for things to do.
1. Circle the categories of things to do.
2. Is each event under the correct category? Do the categories make sense?
3. Does your partner give enough detail about each event?

B PAIRS Can your partner improve his or her event guide? Make suggestions.

6 PROOFREAD

Read your article again. Check your
- spelling
- punctuation
- capitalization

Proofreading tip

Fact-check your writing. Before you finish your event guide. Go online and make sure all of the details about your events are correct.

■ I CAN WRITE ABOUT LOCAL EVENTS.

PUT IT TOGETHER

1 PRESENTATION PROJECT

▶ **A** ▶03-20 Listen or watch. What is the topic of the presentation?

▶ **B** ▶03-21 Listen or watch again. Complete the chart.

Festival	
Location	
Participants (who, how many)	
Activities	

C Read the Presentation Skill. What kinds of information should you pause after?

D Make your own presentation.

Step 1 Find information about a festival in another country. It could be related to a hobby, nature, art, movies, music, or other entertainment. Complete a chart like the one in 1B.

Step 2 Prepare a two-minute presentation about the festival you chose. Bring an item or picture related to the festival.

Step 3 Give your presentation to the class. Remember to use pauses. Answer questions and get feedback.

> ### PRESENTATION SKILL
>
> **Use pauses**
> Pausing after important phrases gives your audience time to think about what you're saying. Think about the most important information in your presentation and pause after you say it so your audience can focus on that point.

How did you do? Complete the self-evaluation on page 165.

2 REFLECT AND PLAN

A Look back through the unit. Check (✓) the things you learned. Highlight the things you need to learn.

Speaking objectives
- ☐ Talk about cultural events
- ☐ Give opinions about TV shows
- ☐ Discuss ways to make life more interesting

Vocabulary
- ☐ Cultural events
- ☐ Describing TV shows

Conversation
- ☐ Disagree with an opinion

Pronunciation
- ☐ Phrases with *of*

Listening
- ☐ Listen for lists of examples

Grammar
- ☐ Superlative adjectives
- ☐ Negative questions
- ☐ Adverbial intensifiers with adjectives

Reading
- ☐ Construct mental images

Writing
- ☐ Categorize

B What will you do to learn the things you highlighted? For example, use your app, review your Student Book, or do other practice. Make a plan.

> ‹ Notes   Done
>
> Review the grammar chart in Lesson 2, page 32.
> _____
> _____
> _____

4

WHAT SHOULD I BUY?

LEARNING GOALS

In this unit, you
- ⊘ give shopping advice
- ⊘ ask to return a purchase
- ⊘ discuss how people shop
- ⊘ read about important possessions
- ⊘ write a complaint

GET STARTED

A Read the unit title and learning goals.

B Look at the photo. What's going on?

C Now read Lan's message. Why do you think she wants to shop now?

LAN PHAM
@LanP

My last few days in New York.
Time to go shopping!

41

LAN PHAM
@LanP

It's my friend Lin's birthday next week. I don't know what to get her!

 1 VOCABULARY Shopping online

A ▶04-01 Read the website. Then listen and repeat the vocabulary words.

SUPER DEALS
Your Online Store for Everything

$12! (+ tax)

Earphones on sale! All your favorite brands!

a shopping cart

a wish list

Apply for a store card! Big savings!

Free shipping with orders over $30!

Use a coupon code and save 10%.

Not satisfied? Returns are easy!

B Use words from the website in 1A to complete the sentences.

1. When you're going to buy something, you put it in your _____ .
2. You can enter a _____ to get 10% off.
3. When you want something, but aren't ready to buy it, put it on your _____ .
4. There is no charge for _____ an item to your house if you spend more than $30.
5. _____ are not a problem. If you don't like something, you can send it back.
6. There are several _____ of earphones. They are all _____ right now.

C PAIRS Describe something you or someone you know has bought online. What was the brand? Was it on sale? Were there taxes? Shipping costs?

I bought a new phone online last week. I had to pay tax on it but no shipping costs.

2 GRAMMAR Embedded *wh-* questions

Embedded *wh-* questions usually come after verbs like *know, remember, see,* and *tell*. You can embed a *wh-* question in a question or statement. The embedded *wh-* question begins with a question word, but it has statement word order.

Direct *wh-* question		Embedded questions		
		Question word	Subject	Verb
What did she buy?	Do you know	what	she	bought?
When is the sale?	Please tell me	when	the sale	is.

We also use question words with infinitive phrases—usually when we're trying to be polite.

	Question word	Infinitive phrase (*to* + verb)
I don't know	where	to look.
Could you tell me	how	to exchange this item?

>> FOR PRACTICE, GO TO PAGE 134

3 CONVERSATION SKILL

A ▶04-02 Read the conversation skill. Listen. Notice how the speakers make suggestions.

Make suggestions

Use expressions like these to make polite suggestions:
Why don't you …
You could try …
You might want to …
Have you thought about …

1. A: I need some new shoes.
   B: You might want to try Mario's. They're having a big sale right now.
2. A: That's my favorite brand of shampoo, but I can't find it in the store anymore.
   B: Have you thought about looking for it online?

B Complete the statements and questions with your own ideas. Say them to a partner and take turns giving each other shopping advice, using language from the conversation skill box.

1. I need to buy a new _____ .
2. Can you recommend a good _____ store?
3. I don't know where to get _____ for my friend's birthday.

4 CONVERSATION

A ▶04-03 Listen or watch. What is Lan's problem?

B ▶04-04 Listen or watch again. Answer the questions.

1. How can Lan search for her friend's wish list?
2. What does Lan decide to buy her friend?
3. What does Ahmet suggest as a way for Lan to save money?

C ▶04-05 FOCUS ON LANGUAGE Listen. Complete the conversation.

> Do you usually buy gifts online or in a store? Are there things you wouldn't buy online?

Lan:	I have to get a gift for a friend, and I'm trying to figure out _____ .
Ahmet:	Is she in the States?
Lan:	Yeah, that's why I want to get it while I'm here—so I don't have to pay shipping from Vietnam.
Ahmet:	That makes sense. Do you have any idea _____ ?
Lan:	No! That's the problem!
Ahmet:	I see. _____ checking for a public wish list.

5 TRY IT YOURSELF

A THINK Make a list of three things that you need or want to buy soon.

B DISCUSS Ask three classmates for advice about an item on your list. Take notes in the chart.

Item			
Where to shop			
How to save money			

A: Do you know where I can buy a pillow?
B: You might want to try Bed-Mart. They have a big selection and a lot of sales.

C ANALYZE Share the advice you got. Did most people suggest buying your items online or not?

☐ I CAN GIVE SHOPPING ADVICE.

LESSON 2 ASK TO RETURN A PURCHASE

LAN PHAM
@LanP

You know that feeling when you buy something, bring it home, and then realize you hate it? 😩 On my way back to the store.

1 VOCABULARY A store return policy

A ▶04-06 Read the store policy. Then listen and repeat the vocabulary words.

RJ's **Store Policy**: Returns

In most cases, you can return **a purchase** for any reason.

It doesn't fit.

It's defective.

I didn't like the color.

I changed my mind.

We do not give cash **refunds**. You may be able to **exchange** your item for one of the same value or receive a **store credit** for the amount you paid. You can spend the credit on any item in the store. **All sales are final** on Red Tag sale items. No returns will be accepted.

All tags must still be attached.

Please have the **receipt** for your item.

B ▶04-07 Listen. Circle the sentence that describes the situation.

1. a. The item is defective.
   b. The item doesn't fit.
2. a. He wants to get a refund.
   b. He wants to exchange the item.
3. a. The skirt doesn't have a tag.
   b. The skirt is on sale.
4. a. The lamp is defective.
   b. She changed her mind.
5. a. He can get a cash refund.
   b. He can get a store credit.
6. a. They are looking at a price tag.
   b. They are looking at a receipt.

C PAIRS Talk about a time you returned something to a store. Why did you return it? Did you get an exchange, a refund, or a store credit?

I returned a sweater that my mom bought me. It didn't fit, so I exchanged it for a smaller one. I had the receipt, so it was no problem.

2 GRAMMAR *Think, imagine,* and *wonder* for requests

Use *think, imagine,* or *wonder* to soften requests and make them more polite.
Think and *imagine* can be followed by *that,* but we usually omit it. The request uses normal statement word order.

		Subject	*Can / Could*	Verb + rest of sentence
Do you think	(that)	I	could	exchange this?
I imagine	(that)	you	can	give me a refund.

Wonder is followed by *if* in polite requests.

		Subject	*Can / Could*	Verb + rest of sentence
I wonder	if	you	could	look up this price for me.

>> FOR PRACTICE, GO TO PAGE 135

3 PRONUNCIATION

Ⓐ ▶04-08 Read and listen to the pronunciation note.

Ⓑ ▶04-09 Listen. Notice the difference in how the letter *x* is pronounced in examples. Then listen and repeat.

> **The prefix ex-**
>
> The letter *x* in the prefix *ex-* can be pronounced /ks/ or /gz/. We pronounce the *x* as /ks/ when *ex-* is stressed, as in *exercise* /ˈéksɚsaɪz/ and when *ex-* is unstressed and followed by a consonant, as in *expire* /ɛkspáɪr/. We pronounce the *x* as /gz/ when *ex-* is unstressed and followed by a vowel, as in *exact* /ɛgzǽkt/.

/ks/			/gz/		
expire	exciting	expression	exactly	example	examine
_____	_____	_____	_____	_____	_____

Ⓒ ▶04-10 Listen. Write these words in the correct box in 3B. Then listen and repeat.

| exam | except | executive | exist | experience | extreme |

4 CONVERSATION

Ⓐ ▶04-11 Listen or watch. Can Lan return or exchange the watch?

Ⓑ ▶04-12 Listen or watch again. Answer the questions.

1. Why does the sales associate talk to the manager?
2. What does the manager say?
3. What will Lan do right after this conversation?

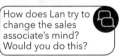

How does Lan try to change the sales associate's mind? Would you do this?

Ⓒ ▶04-13 FOCUS ON LANGUAGE Listen again. Complete the conversation.

Lan:	Hi. I was wondering _____. I bought it here a couple of days ago.
Sales associate:	That shouldn't be any problem. Is it defective?
Lan:	No, no. I just ... I just changed my mind about it.
Sales associate:	OK. Do you have your receipt?
Lan:	Yeah, I do. And the tags are still attached.
Sales associate:	Hmm. Unfortunately, you bought this during our Red Tag sale, and that means all sales are final.
Lan:	Well, do you think _____? Or get a store credit?

5 TRY IT YOURSELF

Ⓐ THINK Think about a time you needed to exchange or return a purchase. What did you buy? Did you want to return or exchange it? Why?

Ⓑ ROLE PLAY Student A: You're a customer. You want to return or exchange the item in 5A. Explain your situation and ask to return the item. Student B: You're a sales associate. Explain the store policy. Will you accept the return?

A: I was wondering if I could return this TV. I have my receipt.
B: Well, according to the store policy, you can only return a TV if it's defective.

Ⓒ EVALUATE Share the results of your conversation. Did Student B allow Student A to return the item? Was Student B's store policy reasonable? Why or why not?

■ I CAN ASK TO RETURN A PURCHASE.

LAN PHAM
@LanP

I just saw a talk about differences in how men and women shop. I think I shop more like a man!

1 BEFORE YOU LISTEN

A Read the information in the chart. Do you enjoy shopping for these things? Have you ever bought any of them online?

Popular Online Shopping Categories

Percentage of internet users who have bought:

FASHION	58%
TRAVEL	55%
BOOKS / MUSIC / PAPER	50%
EVENT TICKETS	41%
ELECTRONICS	40%
BEAUTY AND PERSONAL CARE	38%
FURNITURE, TOOLS, ITEMS FOR THE HOME	29%
VIDEO GAME-RELATED PRODUCTS	27%

B ▶04-14 VOCABULARY Listen. Then listen and repeat. Do you know these words?

market research: the act of collecting information about what people like or need
specific: exact
particular: choosing what you like very carefully
a survey: a set of questions you ask a large number of people in order to find out about their opinions or behavior
confirm: to say or show that something is definitely true
a scan: a medical test in which a machine produces a picture of something inside your body

C Complete the sentences with words from 1B.
1. Companies do _____ to find out if their products will be popular.
2. I do online research about products to _____ what companies say in ads.
3. My sister is very _____ about her clothing. She'll only wear certain styles.
4. A scientist can use a brain _____ to help learn how a person's mind works.
5. The researchers asked shoppers to fill out a _____ with ten questions.
6. I only shop for _____ items. I know exactly what I want.

2 GRAMMAR *While* and *whereas*

Use *while* and *whereas* to contrast actions or ideas. The clause with *while* or *whereas* can come before or after the main clause.

Main clause	*While* or *whereas* clause
Some women get together with friends to shop,	whereas some women like to shop alone.
***While* or *whereas* clause**	**Main clause**
While few people buy groceries online,	large numbers of people buy clothing online.

>> FOR PRACTICE, GO TO PAGE 136

3 LISTENING

Adriana Lopez | TSW Global Speaker Program
Unit 4: Men, women, and shopping

A ▶04-15 Listen or watch. Which statement matches the speaker's point of view?

   a. Men and women will probably always have different shopping behaviors.

   b. The shopping behaviors of men and women will probably change in the future.

B ▶04-16 Read the Listening Skill. Listen or watch again. Complete the definitions.

   1. Men are usually more goal oriented, meaning that they focus on making _____ when shopping.

   2. Women are more likely to make impulse purchases, that is, to _____ they hadn't planned on buying.

> **LISTENING SKILL** Listen for definitions
>
> Sometimes speakers define words as they are speaking. Listen for definitions beginning with *that is* or *meaning*.
> *They often give customers a survey,* **that is**, *a list of questions, to find out what they think.*
> *Companies need to do market research,* **meaning** *that they need to gather information about whether people want or need their product.*

C ▶04-17 Listen or watch again. Circle all correct answers.

   1. What are some traditional male shopping behaviors?

      a. They don't like shopping.

      b. They look for a specific purchase.

      c. They shop with friends.

      d. They look for deals.

   2. What are some traditional female shopping behaviors?

      a. They like shopping.   c. They go to several stores.

      b. They view it as a social activity.   d. They look for deals.

   3. What differences have been found between younger and older men?

      a. Older men like to browse online.   c. Younger men enjoy shopping more.

      b. Older men spend more time looking for bargains.   d. Younger men shop with friends.

D VOCABULARY EXPANSION Read the sentences. What do the underlined expressions mean?

   1. Of course, I'm not describing everyone, but we can make these <u>generalizations</u> about men and women because there are many market research surveys to confirm them.

   2. Differences between men's and women's shopping habits are explained by our history of hunting and gathering. These ancient behaviors still <u>influence</u> us today.

   3. No matter what our <u>ancestors</u> did, these traditional habits appear to be changing.

E PAIRS Compare your answers in 3D.

4 DISCUSSION

A THINK Do you fit the traditional description of male or female shopping behavior? How do you think people's shopping behavior will change in the future?

B DISCUSS In small groups, talk about your ideas in 4A. Take notes about the ways your group thinks people's shopping behavior will change in the future.

I'm really careful when I shop online for electronics. I read reviews and compare prices. I think people will get more particular as they shop online more.

C EVALUATE As a class, discuss the ways you think shopping behaviors will change. Which ideas seem the most likely?

■ I CAN DISCUSS HOW PEOPLE SHOP.

LAN PHAM
@LanP

What's one thing that you would never get rid of? For me, it's an old blanket my grandmother made.

1 BEFORE YOU READ

A PAIRS Do you keep objects from your childhood? Or gifts from a loved one?
Do you have an object that makes you think of a special time or person?

I have an old guitar that my grandfather gave me. I like to play it because ...

 B ▶04-18 VOCABULARY Listen. Then listen and repeat. Do you know these words?

a possession	Identity	remind (someone) of	an heirloom
have sentimental value	pass away	a substitute	associate

>> FOR DEFINITIONS AND PRACTICE, GO TO PAGE 136

2 READ

A PREVIEW Look at the title and the headings. What do you think this article is about?

B ▶04-19 Read and listen to the article. Was your prediction correct?

What would you save?

When you hear about a tragic event, like a fire or a flood, it's natural to feel sad for the people involved. It's also natural to think, "If this happened to me, what would I save?" Many people, like me, would take things that aren't expensive or even very useful. Why? There are a few reasons.

It's a part of me!

5 Sometimes, a possession has been around so long that it becomes an important part of the owner's identity, representing their skills, goals, or
10 experiences.

Jeremy "I am a professional photographer, and I own several expensive, modern cameras. However, I also have a much older
15 camera—it uses film! My father gave it to me years ago when I said I wanted to become a photographer. I took it with me everywhere—it was like a part of my body! My first
20 camera reminds me of when I decided what I wanted to be."

Not "what" but "who"

An heirloom can have sentimental value because it connects us to a loved one
25 who has passed away, becoming a sort of substitute for that person.

Sara "I have a teapot that used to be my grandmother's. For many years, I
would visit my grandmother on
30 Sundays, and she would serve tea from this beautiful teapot. If I was feeling sad or angry about something, talking with my grandmother over tea always helped. She always said, 'Tea makes
35 everything better.' My grandmother passed away two years ago. Now her teapot is on a shelf in my kitchen. It's like a part of her is still with me."

I remember ...

40 Many times, we associate our things with a specific memory. Even if we can't be in that place or time again, we go back there in our minds.

Dana "Five years ago, when I came
45 home from work, I walked up to my front door and heard someone inside my apartment. I ran to the café next door and called the police. A police officer came to the café and said, 'Come with
50 me, please.' We walked into my apartment and my friends jumped up and yelled, 'Happy Birthday' and put a paper crown on my head. I wasn't being robbed—it was a surprise party! Every
55 time I see that paper crown, I laugh."

3 CHECK YOUR UNDERSTANDING

A Read the article again. According to the article, what are three things that make someone want to keep a possession? Circle the correct answer.

   a. They are useful, cost a lot of money, and have sentimental value.

   b. They are useful, connect us to a loved one, and are associated with a bad memory.

   c. They are part of our identity, a substitute for a loved one, and a reminder of a special time.

B Circle the correct answers, according to the article.

   1. Jeremy's old camera ___ .
      a. is a family heirloom.
      b. is part of his identity
      c. doesn't work anymore

   2. Sarah's teapot ___ .
      a. is used every day
      b. is a priceless antique
      c. belonged to her grandmother.

   3. Dana associates her crown with___ .
      a. one special memory
      b. one special person
      c. all of her birthdays

C CLOSE READING Reread lines 1–4. Then choose the correct answers.

   1. What sentence is closest in meaning to the first sentence?
      a. Most people have been in a fire or flood and feel sad about it.
      b. Most people feel sad for others who have had something bad happen to them.
      c. Fires and floods are normal events in many people's lives.

   2. Why does the author use the phrase *like me*?
      a. to say that he is the same as many other people
      b. to say that he is a popular person
      c. to say that he is unusual when compared to other people

D Read the Reading Skill. Reread the descriptions of important possessions. Underline how each person feels today. Then circle the events in the past that help explain why he or she feels that way.

> **READING SKILL**
> **Link the past to the present**
>
> Writers often describe something in the past in detail to explain how they feel today. Look for these details to better understand the writer and his or her meaning.

E PAIRS What is the article about? Summarize the most important ideas. Use your own words.

   The article is about why people value some of their possessions ...

4 MAKE IT PERSONAL

> What are other reasons people become attached to their possessions? 🔍

A What three objects are the most important to you? Complete the chart. Write the object and a short reason or reasons for why it's so important.

Object	Identity	Sentimental value	Memory

B PAIRS Compare your ideas in 4A. Use your notes in the chart to explain why you chose those three objects.

   My first object is my high school swimming award because ...

■ I CAN READ ABOUT IMPORTANT POSSESSIONS.

LAN PHAM
@LanP

A clothing store messed up my online order. I hope they fix the problem soon!

1 BEFORE YOU WRITE

A What do you do when you buy something online and it doesn't work or you are sent the wrong product? Do you complain?

B Read the complaint. What problems did Lan have with her online order?

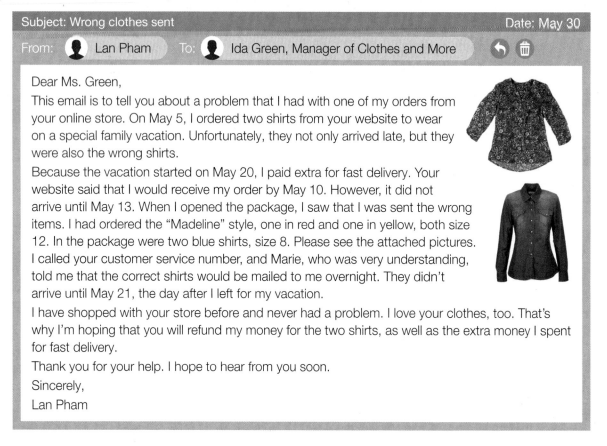

Subject: Wrong clothes sent   Date: May 30

From: Lan Pham   To: Ida Green, Manager of Clothes and More

Dear Ms. Green,

This email is to tell you about a problem that I had with one of my orders from your online store. On May 5, I ordered two shirts from your website to wear on a special family vacation. Unfortunately, they not only arrived late, but they were also the wrong shirts.

Because the vacation started on May 20, I paid extra for fast delivery. Your website said that I would receive my order by May 10. However, it did not arrive until May 13. When I opened the package, I saw that I was sent the wrong items. I had ordered the "Madeline" style, one in red and one in yellow, both size 12. In the package were two blue shirts, size 8. Please see the attached pictures. I called your customer service number, and Marie, who was very understanding, told me that the correct shirts would be mailed to me overnight. They didn't arrive until May 21, the day after I left for my vacation.

I have shopped with your store before and never had a problem. I love your clothes, too. That's why I'm hoping that you will refund my money for the two shirts, as well as the extra money I spent for fast delivery.

Thank you for your help. I hope to hear from you soon.

Sincerely,

Lan Pham

C Reread the complaint. Complete the outline with information from the complaint.

A: Recipient (who the complaint is to) _____
B: Body of letter
    1. Reasons for complaint
        a. _____
        b. _____
    2. Details of complaint
        a. _____
        b. _____
        c. _____
    3. Suggested resolution _____
C: Closing and sender _____

2 FOCUS ON WRITING

Read the Writing Skill. Then circle the polite language that you find in the complaint.

> **WRITING SKILL** Use polite language
>
> Use polite language in a written complaint so that a person or company will be more likely to help. Writers use softening words like *unfortunately* and give compliments when they can to make a complaint sound more polite.

3 PLAN YOUR WRITING

A Think of an item you bought that you had a problem with or use your imagination to think of a new situation. What did you buy? What was the problem with it? How would you like the store to resolve the problem? Take notes in the outline.

> **A: Recipient (who the complaint is to)** _____
> **B: Body of letter**
>   1. Reasons for complaint
>   a. _____
>   b. _____
>   2. Details of complaint
>   a. _____
>   b. _____
>   c. _____
>   3. Suggested resolution _____
> **C: Closing and sender** _____

B PAIRS Talk about your ideas. Suggest ways your partner can improve or add to his or her ideas.

I think your complaint is clear, but you could ...

4 WRITE

Write an email to complain about an item that you bought. Make sure you use polite language in your complaint. Use the complaint in 1B as a model.

> **Writing tip**
>
> Put the important information first. If you put it somewhere in the middle or at the end, the reader might not understand why you are writing.

5 REVISE YOUR WRITING

A PAIRS Exchange emails and read your partner's complaint.
1. Underline the main problem. Is it in the first paragraph?
2. Put a check mark (✓) next to each detail of the problem. Are the details clear?
3. Did your partner use polite language?

B PAIRS Can your partner improve his or her complaint? Make suggestions.

6 PROOFREAD

Read your article again. Check your

- spelling
- punctuation
- capitalization

■ I CAN WRITE A COMPLAINT.

PUT IT TOGETHER

1 PRESENTATION PROJECT

▶ 🎬 **A** ▶04-20 Listen or watch. What is the topic of the presentation?

▶ 🎬 **B** ▶04-21 Listen or watch again. Complete the chart.

Name of store	
Product or service	
Why offer this product or service	
How to attract customers	
Plan to offer quality service	

C Read the Presentation Skill. How do you know when a presenter is excited about a topic. Make a list.

D Make your own presentation.

Step 1 Pretend you are going to open a store. You may provide a service or sell a product. Complete a chart like the one in 1B.

Step 2 Prepare a two-minute presentation about your store. Bring an item or picture related to the product or service you will provide.

Step 3 Give your presentation to the class. Remember to show enthusiasm. Answer questions and get feedback.

> **PRESENTATION SKILL**
>
> **Show enthusiasm**
> It's easier for audience members to pay attention if you are excited about your topic. Use your voice and body language to show enthusiasm.

How did you do? Complete the self-evaluation on page 165.

2 REFLECT AND PLAN

A Look back through the unit. Check (✓) the things you learned. Highlight the things you need to learn.

Speaking objectives
- [ ] Give shopping advice
- [ ] Ask to return a purchase
- [ ] Discuss how people shop

Vocabulary
- [ ] Shopping online
- [ ] A store return policy

Conversation
- [ ] Make suggestions

Pronunciation
- [ ] The prefix -ex

Listening
- [ ] Listen for definitions

Grammar
- [ ] Embedded *wh-* questions
- [ ] *Think, imagine,* and *wonder* for requests
- [ ] *While* and *whereas*

Reading
- [ ] Link the past to the present

Writing
- [ ] Use polite language

B What will you do to learn the things you highlighted? For example, use your app, review your Student Book, or do other practice. Make a plan.

‹ Notes   Done

In the app, do the Lesson 2 Vocabulary practice: A store return policy

_____

_____

_____

5 DO YOU BELONG TO A GYM?

LEARNING GOALS

In this unit, you
- ⊙ talk about health resolutions
- ⊙ describe symptoms and injuries
- ⊙ discuss sleep habits
- ⊙ read about the habits of top athletes
- ⊙ write about bad habits

GET STARTED

A Read the unit title and learning goals.

B Look at the photo. What's going on?

C Now read Ahmet's message. What kind of habits does he want to start?

AHMET TANIR
@AhmetT

I've been thinking about my health lately. Time to start some new habits!

53

AHMET TANIR
@AhmetT

I try to be healthy, but sometimes it's so hard! 😕

 1 VOCABULARY Healthy living

A ▶05-01 **Listen. Then listen and repeat.**

stop drinking soda

get more exercise

drink more water

get more sleep

practice meditation

get regular checkups

eat healthier food

spend time in nature

B ▶05-02 **Listen. What advice is the person giving? Circle the correct answer.**

1. a. get more exercise   b. practice meditation   c. spend time in nature
2. a. stop drinking soda   b. eat healthier food   c. drink more water
3. a. get more sleep   b. get more exercise   c. drink more water
4. a. practice meditation   b. eat healthier food   c. get more exercise
5. a. get regular checkups   b. get more sleep   c. spend time in nature
6. a. drink more water   b. eat healthier food   c. practice meditation
7. a. get regular checkups   b. spend time in nature   c. stop drinking soda
8. a. eat healthier food   b. practice meditation   c. drink more water

C PAIRS **Give an example of how someone could accomplish each of the health resolutions in 1A.**

A: You could stop drinking soda during the week and have it only on weekends.
B: You could get more exercise by walking to work instead of driving.

2 GRAMMAR Past intentions

To talk about things you wanted to do in the past but didn't do, use the past continuous of *go, plan, hope, plan on,* and *think.*
He was going to start his diet, but he didn't.

Use *was about* + infinitive to talk about something that was going to happen very soon but didn't (or hasn't yet).
I was about to leave.

	Was / were	Going / planning / hoping	Infinitive	
I	was	going	to start	my diet this week.
They	were	planning	to drink	more water.
She	was	hoping	to leave	early.
		Planning on / thinking about	**Gerund**	
He	was	planning on	going	out.
I	was	thinking about	joining	the gym.

>> FOR PRACTICE, GO TO PAGE 137

3 CONVERSATION SKILL

(A) ▶05-03 Read the conversation skill. Listen. Notice how the speakers show understanding.

1. **A:** I was planning to run in the park this weekend, but I was too tired.

   B: I know how that is. I'm always tired on the weekends.

2. **A:** I want to eat healthier food, but I love sweets.

   B: I'm the same way.

> **Show understanding**
>
> Use expressions like these to show that you understand how someone feels or that you have had a similar experience:
> *I'm the same way.*
> *I have the same problem.*
> *I know how that is.*
> *I know how you feel.*
> *I know exactly what you mean.*

(B) Complete the statements with your own ideas. Say them to a partner and take turns showing that you understand. Use the language from the conversation skill box.

1. I was planning _____ , but _____ .

2. I was going _____ , but _____ .

4 CONVERSATION

(A) ▶05-04 Listen or watch. What are they talking about?

a. the importance of exercise

b. foods in a healthy diet

c. health habits they'd like to change

(B) ▶05-05 Listen or watch again. Answer the questions.

1. Why does Ahmet want to go on a diet?

2. How does Ahmet's wife make sure she drinks enough water?

3. What does Lan say about her sleeping habits? What does Ahmet say about his?

> Why do you think Ahmet and Lan have trouble keeping their health resolutions? Do you think most people have trouble keeping their health resolutions?

(C) ▶05-06 FOCUS ON LANGUAGE Listen. Complete the conversation.

Lan:	My hotel has a really nice gym. I _____ there every day, but I've been here for a week and I haven't gone once!
Ahmet:	Do you belong to a gym at home?
Lan:	No. I go to yoga classes sometimes, not as often as I should. I'm just so busy all the time.
Ahmet:	I know what you mean. I _____ the gym near my house, but by the time I get home from work, I'm always too tired to go.

5 TRY IT YOURSELF

(A) THINK Make a list of health resolutions or other resolutions that you made but didn't keep.

(B) PAIRS Explain what happened. Why didn't you do what you were planning to do?

A: I was going to take an exercise class, but I haven't done it yet. I'm just so busy.
B: I'm the same way. It's hard to find the time.

(C) ANALYZE Share stories with the class. Determine what are the most common reasons people don't do what they plan to do. Make a list of ideas for overcoming the problems.

■ I CAN TALK ABOUT HEALTH RESOLUTIONS.

LESSON 2   DESCRIBE SYMPTOMS AND INJURIES

AHMET TANIR
@AhmetT

Running is usually good for you … but sometimes it's not!

1 VOCABULARY Symptoms and injuries

A ▶05-07 Listen. Then listen and repeat.

 My feet ache.

 I pulled a muscle.

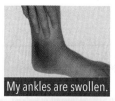 My ankles are swollen.

 My back is sore.

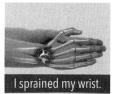 I sprained my wrist.

 My knee hurts.

 I feel exhausted.

 I'm having trouble swallowing.

 I broke my thumb.

 I have a stiff neck.

B Write the statements from 1A in the correct column.

Symptoms	Injuries

C PAIRS Talk about each symptom or injury in 1A. When would or wouldn't you go to the doctor for this problem?

I wouldn't go to the doctor if my feet ached after a long walk.

> In conversation, we often use *me too* and *me neither* to show similarity or agreement.

2 GRAMMAR *So*, *too*, *neither*, and *either*

Use short responses with *so, too, neither,* and *either* to show similarity or agreement.

Verbs other than *be*	To agree with affirmative statements, use *So* + auxiliary verb + subject OR Subject + auxiliary verb + *too*.	To agree with negative statements, use *Neither* + auxiliary verb + subject OR Subject + negative auxiliary verb + *either*.
Present	A: I have a sore back. B: **So do I. / I do, too.**	A: I don't have time to exercise. B: **Neither do I. / I don't either.**
Past	A: I pulled a muscle. B: **So did I. / I did, too.**	A: I didn't get sick last year. B: **Neither did I. / I didn't either.**
Modal	A: I can run pretty fast. B: **So can I. / I can, too.**	A: I can't go to the Fun Run. B: **Neither can I. / I can't either.**
Present perfect	A: I've sprained my ankle twice. B: **So have I. / I have, too.**	A: I've never broken my arm. B: **Neither have I. / I haven't either.**
Be	*So* + *be* + subject OR Subject + *be* + *too*	*Neither* + *be* + subject OR Subject + negative *be* + *either*
	A: I'm exhausted. B: **So am I. / I am, too.**	A: I wasn't at the race. B: **Neither was I. / I wasn't either.**

>> FOR PRACTICE, GO TO PAGE 138

3 PRONUNCIATION

A ▶05-08 Read and listen to the pronunciation note.

B ▶05-09 Listen. Notice how the words in the examples are blended. Then listen and repeat.

So can I.	Neither can I.
So did they.	Neither are they.
So is she.	Neither does she.
So have I.	Neither have you.

C ▶05-10 Listen. Write the phrase you hear.

1. A: Jack couldn't finish the race.
   B: _____ .

2. A: I've never broken a bone.
   B: _____ .

3. A: I can run pretty fast.
   B: _____ .

4 CONVERSATION

A ▶05-11 Listen or watch. What do Marcos and Ahmet decide to do?

B ▶05-12 Listen or watch again. Answer the questions.

1. What is the Fun Run?
2. Who is going on the Fun Run?
3. Why does Marcos decide not to run?

C ▶05-13 FOCUS ON LANGUAGE Listen again. Complete the conversation.

How can you avoid injuries like Marcos's and Ahmet's? How can they recover?

> Marcos: So I guess I can't do the Fun Run.
>
> Ahmet: Well, _____ .
>
> Marcos: Oh, no! What happened to you?
>
> Ahmet: I fell during a practice run and broke my ankle. It got really swollen and was so painful.
>
> Marcos: Oh, man. That's too bad.
>
> Ahmet: I know. I was looking forward to the run. But I am going - to cheer them on. I can at least do that.
>
> Marcos: _____ ! That's a great idea!

5 TRY IT YOURSELF

A THINK Imagine you have a symptom or an injury. How did it happen? How did it feel?

B ROLE PLAY Student A: Tell your partner about your symptom or injury. Student B: Ask questions and show sympathy. Say if you have had a similar experience.

A: My knee hurts.   B: Oh, I'm sorry. What happened to it?

C ANALYZE Report to the class how your partner is feeling and describe the symptoms. Make a list of ideas for treatment. Decide whether the person should go to the doctor.

■ I CAN DESCRIBE SYMPTOMS AND INJURIES.

LESSON 3 DISCUSS SLEEP HABITS

AHMET TANIR
@AhmetT

Did you know that more than 30% of people have trouble falling asleep at night?

1 BEFORE YOU LISTEN

A Read the information in the chart. Which sleep pattern is most similar to yours?

When Do People Sleep?

Australian women
Australian men
Canadian women
Canadian men
Japanese women
Japanese men
Brazilian men
Brazilian women
Spanish men
Spanish women

10 PM 11 PM 12 AM 1 AM 2 AM 3 AM 4 AM 5 AM 6 AM 7 AM 8 AM 9 AM

B ▶05-14 VOCABULARY Listen. Then listen and repeat. Do you know these words?

> **concentrate**: to think very carefully about something you are doing
> **depressed**: very sad
> **overweight**: too heavy
> **an illness**: a sickness or disease
> **a risk**: the chance that something bad might happen
> **diabetes**: a medical condition in which you have too much sugar in your blood
> **heart disease**: an illness affecting the heart
> **rest**: time to relax or sleep

C Answer the questions.

1. What is one thing that can make it difficult to concentrate? _____
2. What should people do if they're feeling a little depressed? _____
3. What's the most important thing people should do if they're overweight? _____
4. What is one thing that can contribute to heart disease or diabetes? _____

D PAIRS Ask and answer the questions in 1C. Do you agree with your partner?

2 GRAMMAR Plans and intentions for the future

Use *intend / mean / plan* + infinitive to talk about plans for the future.

	Intend / mean / plan	Infinitive	
We	intend	to go	to bed early.
He	means	to get up	at 7:00.
They	plan	to wake up	at the same time every day.

>> FOR PRACTICE, GO TO PAGE 139

3 LISTENING

A ▶05-15 Listen or watch. What is the <u>main</u> purpose of the talk?

    a. to explain why people don't get enough sleep

    b. to recommend ways to get a better night's sleep

    c. to describe the benefits of sleeping for eight hours a night

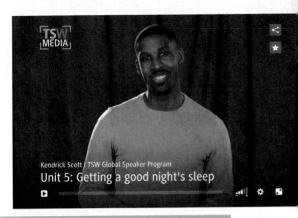

Kendrick Scott | TSW Global Speaker Program
Unit 5: Getting a good night's sleep

B ▶05-16 Read the Listening Skill. Listen or watch again. Complete the comparisons.

    1. They may take _____ to recover from illnesses and have _____ risks of diabetes and heart disease.

    2. Start following this advice immediately. You'll be _____ and _____ . Your mind will be _____ , and you won't fall asleep at work.

> **LISTENING SKILL**
> ### Listen for understood comparisons
>
> Sometimes speakers use comparisons without saying exactly what they are comparing. The listener needs to understand what is being compared from the context.
> *People who don't sleep enough are <u>more likely</u> to get colds.*
> (Understood: They are more likely to get colds than people who do sleep enough.)

C ▶05-17 Listen or watch again. Circle all the correct answers.

    1. What effects of not getting enough sleep does the speaker mention?

        a. trouble concentrating   b. getting injured   c. getting sick   d. getting depressed

    2. What does the speaker recommend instead of taking a nap?

        a. read a book   b. take a walk   c. drink water   d. call a friend

    3. Which things does the speaker say you should *not* do before bed?

        a. eat a big meal   b. take a bath   c. drink water   d. exercise

D VOCABULARY EXPANSION Read the sentences from the talk. What do the underlined expressions mean?

    1. Do you find yourself <u>dozing off</u> in the afternoon when you should be working?

    2. Chances are you don't get enough sleep. <u>Lack</u> of sleep is a big problem nowadays.

    3. Don't sleep on your stomach because it <u>twists</u> your neck.

E PAIRS Compare your answers in 3D.

4 DISCUSSION

A THINK Why do you think lack of sleep is a big problem nowadays? Why is it so hard for people to get enough sleep?

B DISCUSS In small groups, share your ideas in 4A. Take notes about the reasons it is difficult for people to sleep.

Lots of people watch TV at night. They plan to go to bed early, but then they get interested in a program and stay up late.

C EVALUATE Share the ideas you discussed with the class. As a class, decide which three pieces of advice from the talk would be the most useful for most people.

■ I CAN DISCUSS SLEEP HABITS.

LESSON 4 READ ABOUT THE HABITS OF TOP ATHLETES

AHMET TANIR
@AhmetT

I read about how top athletes prepare for competition. I'm no athlete, but I think I could learn a few things from them!

1 BEFORE YOU READ

A PAIRS What is your favorite sport? What skills do athletes need to play it?

I love beach volleyball. Players have to be quick …

B ▶05-18 VOCABULARY Listen. Then listen and repeat. Do you know these words?

peak performance	endurance	vary
a positive attitude	a means to an end	a commitment

>> FOR DEFINITIONS AND PRACTICE, GO TO PAGE 139

2 READ

A PREVIEW Look at the title and the photographs. What do you think this article is about?

B ▶05-19 Read and listen to the article. Was your prediction correct?

REACHING THE PEAK

Yuzuru Hanyu

Serena Williams

Lionel Messi

How can Yuzuru Hanyu do those amazing spins and jumps on the ice? How does Serena Williams win so many tennis tournaments? How is Lionel Messi able to make so many goals? You might think the answer is "practice, practice, practice," but according to a new study from psychologist Brooke Macnamara, you would be wrong. Practice is important for all athletes, of course, but there are
5 other things that make the difference between being good and being one of the best. To reach peak performance, athletes need to watch their diets carefully, get plenty of sleep, and achieve the right state of mind. And when you think about it, those are habits we could all benefit from.

Top athletes know that their bodies need the right fuel. For them, diet is not about body shape—it's about strength, endurance, and energy levels. Of course, their diets vary a lot. Williams eats a lot of nuts, beans,
10 and fruit. Hanyu has soup with pork and soy before every competition. In addition to healthy food, a good diet also includes good hydration. It's important for athletes to get plenty of water and other fluids. The best athletes know that everything they put into their bodies affects their performance.

When athletes train for six hours a day, six days a week, it does a lot of damage to their muscles, and sleep is the only way to repair that damage. Athletes need eight to ten hours of sleep a night—more
15 sleep than the average person. Messi often gets twelve! And many top athletes make an extra effort to get deep, high-quality sleep. A very dark room and cool temperatures are the solution for some. Others use a fan or a white noise machine to block out other sounds. Their specific habits may vary, but all elite athletes know that they need a good night's sleep every night to be at their best.

Finally, the right mental state can make the difference between a good performance and peak
20 performance. Many athletes prepare for competitions by concentrating on positive thoughts or repeating calming words to themselves. They also work hard to keep a positive attitude about the endless hours of training. They make an active effort to enjoy improving their skills rather than just viewing training as a means to an end. And when they are injured, they don't let it get them down but instead focus on what's necessary for recovery. When Hanyu was injured, he continued preparing for
25 the next Olympics with visualization exercises—imagining himself doing his jumps. Many athletes will say that these habits of mental discipline are what put them on top of their game.

For elite athletes, the commitment to peak performance affects every part of their lives. From what they eat for breakfast to when they go to bed at night to how they deal with stress, every habit can make a difference. That's how they make leaping on the ice or slamming the ball over the net look so
30 easy. Most of us are not athletes, but we can apply some of their strategies for success in our own lives.

3 CHECK YOUR UNDERSTANDING

A Read the article again. According to the article, what makes top athletes different from other athletes? Circle the correct answer.

  a. Top athletes are born with more natural ability.

  b. Top athletes develop a variety of habits to improve their performance.

  c. Top athletes spend more hours training than other athletes do.

B Circle the correct answers, according to the article.

  1. Top athletes ___ .

    a. eat mostly fruits and vegetables

    b. have a special meal before competitions

    c. follow different kinds of diets

  2. It's important for athletes to ___ .

    a. get eight to ten hours of sleep

    b. take naps between training sessions

    c. sleep in cool temperatures

  3. When Hanyu was injured, he ___ .

    a. focused on eating a healthy diet

    b. practiced skating by picturing himself jumping

    c. used meditation to relax

C CLOSE READING Reread lines 19–26. Then choose the correct answers.

  1. What is shown by the words *rather than* and *instead*?

    a. comparison   b. contrast   c. addition

  2. Which sentence best summarizes the idea of the paragraph?

    a. They like to improve their skills and try not to get injured while training.

    b. They focus on training and recovering because that is how they can win.

    c. They try to have a good attitude when training and recovering from injuries.

D Read the Reading Skill. Go back to the article and underline the concluding sentences in paragraphs 2, 3, and 4. What is the main idea of each paragraph?

> **READING SKILL Notice concluding sentences**
>
> Writers often finish a paragraph with a sentence that summarizes the main idea. This concluding sentence helps readers focus on what was important about the information presented earlier in the paragraph.

E PAIRS What is the article about? Summarize the most important ideas. Use your own words.

The article is about how top athletes ...

What are some habits of your favorite athlete?

4 MAKE IT PERSONAL

A Make notes about some of your own habits in the chart. How do these habits affect your performance in class, at work, or in any sports you play?

Food / Water	Sleep	Attitude

B PAIRS Compare your ideas in 4A. Explain how your habits affect your performance.

I'm pretty careful about eating healthy food, and I think that helps me ...

■ I CAN READ ABOUT THE HABITS OF TOP ATHLETES.

LESSON 5   WRITE ABOUT BAD HABITS

AHMET TANIR
@AhmetT

I'm trying to break my habit of eating sweets. It was going well until Ed brought cookies into the office!

1 BEFORE YOU WRITE

A Do you have any bad habits that affect your health? How do you try to change them?

B Read the blog post. What examples of bad habits does it mention?

Home | About Me | Health | Family | Work   🔍 *Search*

Let's break those bad habits!   Posted on June 13

The Modern Life of
DAVE TANNER

My alarm clock rings. It's 6:30 A.M., and I promised myself I was going to start going to the gym before work. But I hate getting up early, so I roll over and close my eyes …

We all have bad habits that we struggle to overcome. Maybe, like me, you don't exercise enough or you eat unhealthy foods. Many people watch too much TV.

Archive
January (5)
February (6)
March (5)
April (7)
May (7)
June (3)

We all know that these habits are unhealthy, so the question is: Why are bad habits so hard to break, and what can we do about it?

First, you have to think about why bad habits start in the first place. Many bad habits give us pleasure or enjoyment. For example, eating delicious food is a pleasurable experience, even when the food has too much fat and sugar. Some bad habits take our minds off stressful problems we may have. Watching TV for hours is a way to avoid thinking about what's happening in your life. And some bad habits start because the good habit seems unpleasant or difficult. For me, getting up early and exercising just doesn't seem fun at all, so I avoid it.

How do we begin to break a bad habit? One way is to replace the bad habit with a good one. Instead of buying unhealthy foods, fill your refrigerator with healthy snacks that you enjoy. Instead of watching TV, learn a new hobby, like knitting or photography, that can focus your mind on positive things and help you de-stress.

As for me, I've decided to take a kickboxing class after work. I won't have to get up early, and it sounds like a lot more fun than a treadmill! Breaking a bad habit is never easy, but when you succeed, it not only makes you physically healthier, but it also makes you feel great about yourself. Let's do this!

Leave a Reply

[Enter your comment here…]

C Read the blog post again. Complete the chart with information from the post.

Bad Habits	→	Why they're hard to break	→	What to do about them

2 FOCUS ON WRITING

Read the Writing Skill. Underline the hook in the blog post.

3 PLAN YOUR WRITING

A Think of a bad habit that you have or someone you know has. What is the bad habit? Why is it hard to break this bad habit? What can someone do to break the bad habit? Take notes in the chart.

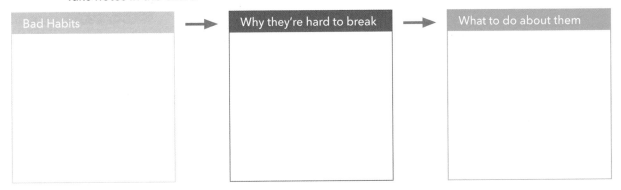

Bad Habits		Why they're hard to break		What to do about them

B PAIRS Talk about your ideas. Suggest ways your partner can improve or add to his or her ideas.

I think you explain the bad habit well, but you should include ...

4 WRITE

Write a blog post to explain a bad habit. Make sure you use a hook that the reader can relate to. Use the blog post in 1B as a model.

5 REVISE YOUR WRITING

A PAIRS Exchange blog posts and read your partner's description of a bad habit.

1. Underline the hook. Can many readers relate to it?
2. Put a check mark (✓) next to examples of why someone has this bad habit. Is the reason clear?
3. Circle the suggestion(s) for what to do about the bad habit. Is it a good idea that anyone can do?

Revising tip

Understand the difference between revising and proofreading. When we revise, we change anything that can make the text clearer or more interesting to the reader. These can include big or small changes. When we proofread, we look for problems in spelling or grammar and mark them.

B PAIRS Can your partner improve his or her blog post? Make suggestions.

6 PROOFREAD

Read your blog post again. Check your

- spelling
- punctuation
- capitalization

■ I CAN WRITE ABOUT BAD HABITS.

PUT IT TOGETHER

1 PRESENTATION PROJECT

A ▶05-20 Listen or watch. What is the topic of the presentation?

B ▶05-21 Listen or watch again. Complete the chart.

Problem	Home remedy	Would the speaker try it?

C Read the Presentation Skill. What are examples of visual aids? Make a list.

D Make your own presentation.

Step 1 Find information about home remedies. Think about whether you would try each one. Complete a chart like the one in 1B.

Step 2 Prepare a two-minute presentation about home remedies. Remember to include large visual aids. Bring items or pictures related to them.

Step 3 Give your presentation to the class. Answer questions and get feedback.

> **PRESENTATION SKILL**
>
> **Use large visual aids**
> Visual aids, like pictures or charts, make a presentation easier to understand and keep the audience interested. Use visual aids that are large enough for everyone in the audience to see.

How did you do? Complete the self-evaluation on page 165.

2 REFLECT AND PLAN

A Look back through the unit. Check (✓) the things you learned. Highlight the things you need to learn.

Speaking objectives
- [ ] Talk about health resolutions
- [ ] Describe symptoms and injuries
- [ ] Discuss sleep habits

Vocabulary
- [ ] Healthy living
- [ ] Symptoms and injuries

Conversation
- [ ] Show understanding

Pronunciation
- [ ] Blending phrases with *so* and *neither*

Listening
- [ ] Listen for understood comparisons

Grammar
- [ ] Past intentions
- [ ] *So, too, neither,* and *either*
- [ ] Plans and intentions for the future

Reading
- [ ] Notice concluding sentences

Writing
- [ ] Use a hook

B What will you do to learn the things you highlighted? For example, use your app, review your Student Book, or do other practice. Make a plan.

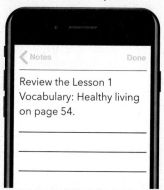

Notes / Done

Review the Lesson 1 Vocabulary: Healthy living on page 54.

6 HAS THE CRIMINAL BEEN CAUGHT?

LEARNING GOALS

In this unit, you
- ⊘ describe a crime
- ⊘ talk about law and order
- ⊘ discuss crime-solving technology
- ⊘ read about Sherlock Holmes
- ⊘ write about a crime

GET STARTED

A Read the unit title and the learning goals.

B Look at the photo. What's going on?

C Now read Marcos' message. Why do you think he finds true crime shows fascinating?

MARCOS ALVES
@MarcosA

My favorite show is on tonight. It's a true crime show—they're so fascinating!

65

MARCOS ALVES
@MarcosA

Stayed up too late watching a true crime show last night. I just had to know how it ended!

1 VOCABULARY Crime and criminals

A ▶06-01 Read the poster. Then listen and repeat the vocabulary words.

TRUE CRIME STORIES

MONA LISA THEFT

On August 21, 1911, an art **thief** walked into the Louvre Museum in Paris and **stole** the *Mona Lisa*. At first no one noticed the **theft**. The man just cut the famous painting out of its frame and walked out with it under his clothing. It took the French police more than two years to find the thief and the painting.

THE GREAT TRAIN ROBBERY

In 1963, a **gang** of 15 **robbers** got away with over $4 million when they carried out a complicated train **robbery** in the UK. Working together, they stole 120 bags of money off the train in 15 minutes.

JOHN PAUL GETTY III KIDNAPPING

Seventeen-year-old John Paul Getty III was the grandson of the richest man in the world when he was **kidnapped** in Rome in 1973. His father refused to pay at first, but eventually he gave the **kidnappers** $2.9 million and the teenager was returned.

JACK THE RIPPER MURDERS

Jack the Ripper is the name given to a **murderer** who **killed** five women in London in 1888. Police never caught him, and some people think he committed six other **murders** around the same time. Today thousands of tourists visit the scenes of his crimes.

B Complete the chart with the bold words in 1A.

People	Crimes	Actions

C PAIRS Talk about a crime that you've heard about in real life or on a TV show. Use at least two of the words from 1A.

There was a robbery at Len's Jewelry Store a few weeks ago. I saw it on the news …

2 GRAMMAR Past perfect

Use the past perfect to talk about an action that occurred before another time in the past.

	Had	Past participle	
The police discovered that the thief	had	taken	the painting.
Before the robbery, the gang	had	dug	a tunnel to the bank.

Notes
- The past perfect is sometimes used with *before, after, by the time*, and *when*.
  By the time police arrived, the robbers had already left.
- We often use contractions with subject pronouns and *had* with the past perfect.
  They**'d** robbed another bank earlier that week.
- We also use the contraction *hadn't* with negative past perfect sentences.
  They didn't stop the thief because they **hadn't** noticed the theft yet.

>> FOR PRACTICE, GO TO PAGE 140

3 CONVERSATION SKILL

A ▶06-02 Read the conversation skill. Listen. Notice how the speaker tries to keep the listener interested.

A: A guy robbed a store yesterday, and dropped the money on the way out the door.

B: You're kidding!

A: It gets better–he also dropped his ID!

Keep your listener interested
When you tell a story, use expressions like these to keep your listener interested: *You're not going to believe …* *It gets better …* *Wait until I tell you …*

B Complete Student A's part of the conversations. Then practice the conversations with a partner.

1. A: Wait until I tell you what I saw on the other day. I saw _____ !

   B: Wow! That's amazing!

2. A: You're not going to believe what my friend did. He _____ !

   B: I can't believe that!

4 CONVERSATION

A ▶06-03 Listen or watch. What are they talking about?

a. a series of bank robberies

b. the details of a bank robbery

c. how a bank robber got caught

B ▶06-04 Listen or watch again. Answer the questions.

1. Why did the robbers pretend to be working near the bank?

2. How long did they spend taking the money?

3. What is Marcos going to tell Leti about?

How does Leti feel about true crime shows? Do you like shows about crimes?

C ▶06-05 FOCUS ON LANGUAGE Listen. Complete the conversation.

Marcos: Well, when the bank employees came to work Monday morning, they didn't even know there _____ a robbery. Everything seemed fine. Then they opened the vault, and it was completely empty!

Leti: What? How is that possible? Didn't they have alarms?

Marcos: They did, but the robbers _____ a guard and forced him to turn off the alarm on Friday night.

5 TRY IT YOURSELF

A THINK Think about a crime story you read about or saw on TV. Take notes about what happened the day of the crime and what had happened before.

B PAIRS Tell the story. Ask and answer questions about the crime.

A: I read that a couple came home, and thieves had stolen all of their furniture.

B: Did the police catch the thieves?

C COMPARE Tell your story to the class. Which is the scariest? Which is most unusual?

■ I CAN DESCRIBE A CRIME.

LESSON 2 / TALK ABOUT LAW AND ORDER

MARCOS ALVES
@MarcosA

Some criminals just aren't very smart.
You'll never believe what this one guy did!

1 VOCABULARY The legal process

A ▶06-06 Listen. Then listen and repeat.

> **a detective**: a police officer whose job is to find out who has committed a crime
> **arrest**: when the police take someone away because they think he or she has done something illegal
> **a victim**: a person who has been hurt or killed by someone
> **a suspect**: someone who the police think may have committed a crime
> **jail / prison**: a place where criminals are sent to stay as punishment
> **a judge**: the person in control of a court who decides if criminals should be punished
> **a lawyer**: someone whose job is to advise people about the law and speak for them in court
> **a witness**: someone who tells a court what he or she knows about a crime
> **a sentence**: a punishment that a judge gives to someone who is guilty of a crime
> **a prisoner**: someone in prison or jail

B ▶06-07 Listen. Who is speaking? Write the correct words from the box.

| a detective | a judge | a lawyer | a prisoner | a suspect | a victim | a witness |

1. _____   3. _____   5. _____   7. _____
2. _____   4. _____   6. _____

C PAIRS Use the words in 1A to describe something you've read about or seen on TV.

I've seen lots of detective shows because my mom loves them. They always arrest the criminal!

2 GRAMMAR Present perfect passive

Use the present perfect passive to talk or ask about things that have already happened or haven't happened yet. These sentences sometimes include a *by* phrase that tells who did the action.

Statements—things that have already happened				
	Has / have	*(Already)*	*Been*	Past participle
The video	has	(already)	been	seen	by millions of people.
The thieves	have			arrested.

Statements—things that haven't happened yet				
	Hasn't / haven't	*Been*	Past participle	*(Yet)*
The painting	hasn't	been	returned	yet.
The other robbers	haven't		caught	

Questions				
Has / Have	Subject	*Been*	Past participle	
Have	the suspects	been	questioned	by the new detective?

Note: The passive focuses on the receiver of the action.

>> FOR PRACTICE, GO TO PAGE 141

3 PRONUNCIATION

A ▶06-08 Read and listen to the pronunciation note.

B ▶06-09 Listen. Notice how -se is pronounced. Then listen and repeat.

/z/: because, surprise, please, lose

/s/: release, defense, promise, worse

C ▶06-10 Listen. Circle the word in each group that has a different sound of -se.

1. ro*se*, pau*se*, ca*se*, supervi*se*
2. purpo*se*, suppo*se*, decrea*se*, expen*se*
3. choo*se*, fal*se*, loo*se*, nur*se*
4. refu*se*, advi*se*, exerci*se*, era*se*

4 CONVERSATION

A ▶06-11 Listen or watch. What are they talking about?

a. why the robbers participated in the bank robbery

b. how the lawyer helped the robber who got caught

c. what happened to one of the robbers and the guard

B ▶06-12 Listen or watch again. Answer the questions.

1. How did the robber get caught?
2. Why did the guard go to jail?
3. Why did the guard get a shorter sentence?

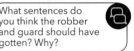
What sentences do you think the robber and guard should have gotten? Why?

C ▶06-13 FOCUS ON LANGUAGE Listen. Complete the conversation.

Marcos:	Not long after the video went up, he had two detectives knocking at his door, and they arrested him.
Leti:	You're kidding. And have the rest of the robbers _____ , too?
Marcos:	Nope. They only caught the one guy. They're still looking for them. And the rest of the money _____ yet.

5 TRY IT YOURSELF

A PAIRS Choose one of the crimes. Work together to create a story about it. Take notes.

What happened?	What hasn't happened yet?

Jewelry Store Robbery— Hundreds of diamonds stolen!

Escape from Newton Jail— Police searching for 7 prisoners

B GROUPS Meet with another pair to tell your stories. Ask and answer questions about what has and hasn't happened yet.

A: Have the robbers been caught yet?

B: No, they haven't. The police have interviewed some witnesses, but they haven't found the suspects yet. And the diamonds haven't been found, either.

C EVALUATE Share your stories with the class. Who told the most interesting story? Why?

☐ I CAN TALK ABOUT LAW AND ORDER.

LESSON 3 DISCUSS CRIME-SOLVING TECHNOLOGY

MARCOS ALVES
@MarcosA

It's amazing how real-life crime-solving technology is catching up to TV!

1 BEFORE YOU LISTEN

A ▶06-14 VOCABULARY Listen. Then listen and repeat.

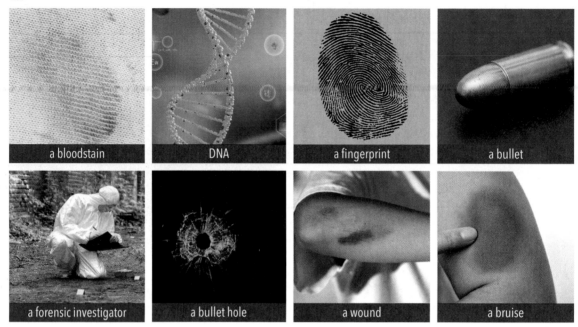

a bloodstain	DNA	a fingerprint	a bullet
a forensic investigator	a bullet hole	a wound	a bruise

B Write the correct word from 1A next to each definition.

1. a cut made in your skin by something such as a knife or bullet _____
2. a small piece of metal that comes out of a gun _____
3. a person who uses science to try to find out what happened in a crime _____
4. a substance in the cells of your body that carries genetic information _____
5. a mark that a finger makes _____
6. a mark made by blood _____
7. a circular shape left after someone shoots a gun _____
8. a mark left on the skin after a hit or other injury _____

C PAIRS Discuss the kinds of information that investigators might get from the items in 1A.

A: A blood stain might tell them where a crime happened.
B: True. And it might also tell them how badly someone was hurt.

2 GRAMMAR Do / did as a verb substitute

Use *do* or *did* to replace verbs or verb phrases instead of repeating them.

	Verb phrase		Do / don't
On TV, DNA samples	come back immediately,	but in real life, they	**don't**.
Fingerprints don't usually	lead straight to the criminal,	but sometimes they	**do**.
Nowadays, we don't	need a large DNA sample,	but in the old days, we	**did**.

3 LISTENING

A ▶06-15 Listen or watch. Which statement matches the speaker's point of view?

a. The forensic science you see on TV is nothing like real forensic science.

b. Real forensic science is getting closer to what you see on TV shows.

c. Real forensic science has gotten more advanced than what you see on TV.

TSW MEDIA

David Cruz | TSW Global Speaker Program
Unit 6: Forensic technology: TV or reality?

B ▶06-16 Read the Listening Skill. Listen or watch again. Complete the sentences with contrast words.

> **LISTENING SKILL** Listen for contrasts
>
> Sometimes speakers signal a contrast by using words such as:
> *nevertheless   however   in contrast*

1. On TV, fingerprints often lead straight to the criminal, but in reality, most fingerprints usually don't. _____ , thanks to advances in technology, there are lots of new developments in forensics that are just as cool as what you see on TV.

2. You already know that scientists can use DNA samples to identify specific people. _____ , that's only useful if a suspect's DNA can be compared to crime scene evidence.

C ▶06-17 Listen or watch again. Check (✓) all the forensic technologies that the speaker mentions.

☐ lasers that can analyze small pieces of glass
☐ computer programs that can match criminals' faces to police records
☐ photography that can track high-speed bullets
☐ cameras that can show damage beneath the skin of a victim
☐ cameras that can analyze blood stains
☐ DNA tests that can tell age, ethnic background, and family members
☐ DNA tests that can provide information about people's habits

D VOCABULARY EXPANSION Read the sentences from the talk. What do the underlined expressions mean?

1. In some ways, the TV shows aren't <u>realistic</u> at all. For example, on TV, DNA tests come back from the lab immediately, but in real life, they can take two weeks.

2. Thanks to advances in technology, there are lots of new <u>developments</u> in forensics that are just as cool as what you see on TV.

3. They can see damage beneath a person's skin, before it's visible to <u>the naked eye</u>.

E PAIRS Compare your answers in 3D.

4 DISCUSSION

A THINK How has forensic technology changed crime solving in the last 50 years? Make a list.

B DISCUSS Share your ideas in small groups. Then discuss how you think technology will change crime solving in the future.

A: In the old days, they didn't have criminal records stored on computers, but now they do.
B: Yeah, and in the future, they'll be able to find that information even more quickly.

C EVALUATE Share the group's ideas about the future of crime solving. Which developments do you think will have the biggest effect on crime solving?

☐ I CAN DISCUSS CRIME-SOLVING TECHNOLOGY.

MARCOS ALVES
@MarcosA

Just read an article about Sherlock Holmes. I had no idea how much influence he had on the real world!

1 BEFORE YOU READ

A PAIRS Do you like detective stories or police shows? Why or why not? What do you know about Sherlock Holmes?

I like shows about detectives because ...   I think Sherlock Holmes was ...

B ▶06-18 VOCABULARY Listen. Then listen and repeat. Do you know these words?

figure out	catch red-handed	accuse	a technique
analysis	influence	preserve	rigorous

>> FOR DEFINITIONS AND PRACTICE, GO TO PAGE 142

2 READ

A PREVIEW Look at the title and the photographs. What do you think the article is about?

B ▶06-19 Read and listen to the article. Was your prediction correct?

𝒜 Fictional Detective & REAL FORENSICS

A woman walks into a detective's office. The detective takes one look at her and says, "I see that you work at the factory in Smithfield." The woman is amazed as he explains that he has figured it out from the mud on her shoe and the color of her dress. But we in the audience
5 aren't surprised. The detective is Sherlock Holmes, and his remarkable skills have been entertaining us since 1892, first in the books by Sir Arthur Conan Doyle, and in movies and television shows ever since. Everybody loves Sherlock Holmes. But what you may not realize is that even though he is a fictional character, he played a big role in the real
10 history of forensic science.

Back when Conan Doyle started writing, criminals were usually arrested because they were caught red-handed or because they were accused by a witness. But because cities were getting busier and more crowded, crime was increasing. Conan Doyle studied medicine, and
15 he believed that applying rigorous scientific methods to solving crimes could help authorities identify more criminals. So he wrote stories in which his Sherlock Holmes character used the latest techniques. And in some areas, Conan Doyle was way ahead of his time.

One way that Conan Doyle predicted real forensics was in his
20 character's use of fingerprints. At that time, some police departments used a method for identifying criminals that involved measuring twelve characteristics of the body, like the length of the arm or the distance between the mouth and nose. Other departments used fingerprinting. Conan Doyle had Sherlock use fingerprint analysis in the story *The*
25 *Sign of the Four* in 1890, and he made the right choice. London's police force began using fingerprint identification in 1901.

Conan Doyle was also ahead of his time when it came to typewriter analysis. In the 1891 story *A Case of Identity*, Sherlock
30 Holmes solves a case because he is able to identify the specific machine that a typewritten letter came from. The amazing thing is that Conan Doyle wrote this story three years before the first time that
35 typewriter analysis was used in court—and around forty years before the FBI began using it officially.

Sherlock Holmes and his creator didn't just predict new developments; they actually
40 influenced forensic scientists. The French detective Edmond Locard, who started the first forensics lab in the 1900s, was such a big fan that he asked his police science students to read the stories to understand
45 the importance of preserving a crime scene.

>>

> Much of what Sherlock Holmes could do was not realistic—even the best
detectives can't just look at a person and guess what he or she ate for breakfast.
But Conan Doyle and his hero predicted forensics in surprising ways. And all you
have to do is turn on the TV to see that our fascination with Sherlock Holmes, and
50 with forensic science in general, is still going strong more than 100 years later.

3 CHECK YOUR UNDERSTANDING

A Read the article again. According to the article, why are the Sherlock Holmes stories important? Circle the correct answer.

a. They invented fingerprint and handwriting analysis.

b. They predicted and influenced forensic science.

c. They have entertained us for more than 100 years.

B Complete the sentences with information from the article.

1. At the time Arthur Conan Doyle started writing, criminals were usually caught red-handed or because _____ .

2. Unlike many police departments, Holmes used _____ to identify criminals, instead of _____ .

3. Conan Doyle _____ Locard with his ideas about _____ .

C CLOSE READING Reread lines 27–37. Then answer the question.

1. What is the sequence of events? Number them in order.

___ The FBI began using typewriter analysis.

___ Sherlock Holmes used typewriter analysis in a story.

___ Typewriter analysis was used for the first time in court.

D Read the Reading Skill. Go back to the article. Identify two examples of Sherlock Holmes being ahead of his time and one example of his influence on forensic scientists.

> **READING SKILL Identify examples**
>
> Writers include examples to illustrate their ideas and make them clear. Sometimes examples are introduced with phrases such as *like* or *for example*, but often they are not. They may just be specific stories that come after the general idea that they are illustrating.

E PAIRS What is the article about? Summarize the most important ideas in your own words.

The article is about how Sherlock Holmes ...

> How else did Sherlock Holmes influence real forensics?

4 MAKE IT PERSONAL

A Who is your favorite fictional character? How has he or she influenced you or others? Take notes in the chart.

Character	Important actions or personality traits	Influence on you or others

B PAIRS Compare your ideas in 4A.

My favorite character is Spider-Man. He's a teenager who ...

▢ I CAN READ ABOUT SHERLOCK HOLMES.

MARCOS ALVES
@MarcosA

When I read some crime stories, I have to wonder what people are thinking.

1 BEFORE YOU WRITE

A Have you read newspaper articles about crimes? What information is important to include in an article about a crime?

B Read the newspaper article about a local crime. What crime was committed?

Middletown News

POLICE PUZZLED BY GREEN GOLF BALLS

Middletown Police are investigating a series of incidents that occurred in Davis Park downtown. According to Police Chief May Fowler, one or more people have been playing golf in the park after the park closes and leaving behind dozens of green-colored golf balls.

Fowler said the incidents occurred over the last three nights. The Middletown Parks Department (MPD) staff arrived at the 20-acre park, which is located across from the town hall, and found the grounds covered with approximately 200 golf balls—all green in color. The Parks Department staff arrives at Davis Park every morning at 5:30 a.m. to empty the garbage cans, perform landscaping duties, and set up for any events that day.

"The Parks Department staff doesn't have time to pick up all of these golf balls, and no one is supposed to be in the park after closing time anyway," Fowler said.

The golf balls are not only a waste of time for the MPD, but they also pose a danger for users of the park who run and bike through the park. Yesterday one early morning jogger tripped and hurt his ankle because he didn't see the ball in the grass.

Chief Fowler reported that officers have found several pieces of evidence, including a golf club, and are processing them for fingerprints. The charges could include vandalism (damaging public property) and littering. The police are not planning to arrest anyone— they just want the golfing to stop.

---

2 FOCUS ON WRITING

A Read the Writing Skill. Underline the information in the article: who do police think committed the crime; what was the crime; when was the crime committed; where was the crime committed; how was the crime committed.

> **WRITING SKILL** Use the 5 Ws and *how*
>
> In a news story, always include the 5 Ws—*who*, *what*, *when*, *where*, *why*—and *how*. These are the most important facts, and they are usually presented at the beginning of a news story. Without these facts, the reader may not understand the news story correctly.

B Read the newspaper article again. Complete the chart with information about the crime.

Who?	What?	When?	Where?	Why?	How?
Any other important details					

3 PLAN YOUR WRITING

A Think of a crime that you saw on the news or a TV show or use your imagination to think of your own idea. What are the 5 Ws of the crime? Complete the chart with information about the crime.

Who?	What?	When?	Where?	Why?	How?
Any other important details					

B PAIRS Talk about your ideas. Suggest ways your partner can improve or add to his or her ideas.

Your crime story is interesting, but you should include information about ...

4 WRITE

Write about a crime that you saw on the news or a TV show or your own idea. Make sure you include information about the 5 Ws and also other important details that the reader should know. Use the newspaper article in 1B as a model.

5 REVISE YOUR WRITING

A PAIRS Exchange articles and read your partner's story.

1. Underline the 5 Ws. Are the 5 Ws all near the beginning of the article?
2. Are the 5 Ws written in a way that is easy to understand?
3. Put a check mark (✓) next to the other important details. Are all the details included important to the story or not?

> **Revising tip**
> Review your writing multiple times. Each time look at a different specific thing.

B PAIRS Can your partner improve his or her newspaper article? Make suggestions.

6 PROOFREAD

Read your newspaper article again. Check your

- spelling
- punctuation
- capitalization

■ I CAN WRITE ABOUT A CRIME.

PUT IT TOGETHER

1 PRESENTATION PROJECT

A ▶06-20 Listen or watch. What is the topic of the presentation?

_____

B ▶06-21 Listen or watch again. Answer the questions.

1. What were the criminals trying to do?
   Criminal 1: _____
   Criminal 2: _____
2. What mistakes did they make?
   Criminal 1: _____
   Criminal 2: _____

C Read the Presentation Skill. How can you practice making eye contact?

D Make your own presentation.

Step 1 Find information about criminals who made mistakes.

- What were the criminals trying to do?
- What mistakes did they make?

Step 2 Prepare a two-minute presentation about criminals who made mistakes. Bring an item or picture that is related to the mistakes.

Step 3 Give your presentation to the class. Remember to make eye contact with your classmates. Answer questions and get feedback.

> **PRESENTATION SKILL**
>
> **Make eye contact**
> People in an audience pay more attention when a speaker is connecting with them. Make eye contact for a few seconds with several people in the audience to show that you are focused on them and to keep their attention.

How did you do? Complete the self-evaluation on page 165.

2 REFLECT AND PLAN

A Look back through the unit. Check (✓) the things you learned. Highlight the things you need to learn.

Speaking objectives
- ☐ Describe a crime
- ☐ Talk about law and order
- ☐ Discuss crime-solving technology

Vocabulary
- ☐ Crime and criminals
- ☐ The legal process

Conversation
- ☐ Keep your listener interested

Pronunciation
- ☐ The letters -se

Listening
- ☐ Listen for contrasts

Grammar
- ☐ Past perfect
- ☐ Present perfect passive
- ☐ Do / did as a verb substitute

Reading
- ☐ Identify examples

Writing
- ☐ Use the 5 Ws and how

B What will you do to learn the things you highlighted? For example, use your app, review your Student Book, or do other practice. Make a plan.

> Notes   Done
>
> Review the grammar chart in Lesson 1, page 66.
> _____
> _____
> _____
> _____

7 DID YOU SEE WHAT SHE'S WEARING?

GET STARTED

A Read the unit title and the learning goals.

B Look at the photo. What's going on?

C Now read Ed's message. Do you watch award shows?

ED MILLER
@EdM

The awards are on tonight. Can't wait to see if *Circle of Kings* won something!

ED MILLER
@EdM

Watching the red carpet interviews. There are some pretty interesting outfits this year!

1 VOCABULARY Clothing verbs and adjectives

A ▶07-01 **Listen and repeat.**

Verbs related to clothing

zip up	take off	put on	tie	button

Adjectives to describe clothing

tight	loose	long-sleeved	short-sleeved	sleeveless

floral	striped	plaid	polka-dotted	solid blue

B Write short answers to the questions.

1. Did you zip up a clothing item this morning? Which one? _____
2. What clothing item do you take off first when you get home? _____
3. Is anyone in your class wearing something floral, striped, or plaid? _____
4. Do you prefer wearing tight clothing or loose clothing? _____
5. Do you prefer wearing long-sleeved, short-sleeved, or sleeveless shirts? _____

C PAIRS Ask and answer the questions in 1B.

2 GRAMMAR Reduced defining relative clauses

Relative clauses with *be* + verb + *-ing* can be shortened by deleting *who* or *that* and the verb *be*.			
Full	I see a guy	**who is** tying his shoe	over there.
Reduced		tying his shoe	
Full	Do you know the woman	**that is** talking to Maria?	
Reduced		talking to Maria?	
Full	The people	**who are** standing in the back	look bored.
Reduced		standing in the back	
Full	He bumped into a woman	**who was** holding a glass.	
Reduced		holding a glass.	

>> FOR PRACTICE, GO TO PAGE 143

3 PRONUNCIATION

A ▶07-02 Read and listen to the pronunciation note.

B ▶07-03 Listen. Notice the emphatic stress on the words with capital letters.

Her dress is GORgeous!   Of COURSE I am.

C ▶07-04 Listen. Underline the words with emphatic stress. Then listen again and repeat.

A: Aren't you freezing in that light jacket? It's cold.

B: Yes, but it was warm when I left home. The weather is crazy.

4 CONVERSATION

A ▶07-05 Listen or watch. What are they talking about?

B ▶07-06 Listen or watch again. Answer the questions.

1. What is Stella Davina wearing?
2. What does Amanda Morgan do in the video Paula is watching?
3. What does Ed realize about Paula's video?

C ▶07-07 FOCUS ON LANGUAGE Listen. Complete the conversation.

Paula:	Who is that woman _____ ? Her dress is gorgeous.
Ed:	Uh, which one?
Paula:	The blonde woman _____ the guy in the plaid jacket.

Why does Paula like awards shows? Do you like awards shows? Why or why not?

5 TRY IT YOURSELF

A THINK Student A: Write names for Picture A. Student B: Write names for Picture B.

_____   _____

B PAIRS Ask and answer questions about the people in your partner's picture. Student A: Ask about the person by describing something he or she is doing. Student B: Ask a question to be sure you understand. Then write the names.

A: Who's the woman wearing the floral dress?   A: Yeah.

B: The one holding a microphone?   B: That's Kay. K-A-Y.

C EVALUATE Tell the class your opinion of the people's clothing.

■ I CAN TALK ABOUT PEOPLE'S CLOTHES.

LESSON 2　　TALK ABOUT CLOTHING REPAIRS

ED MILLER
@EdM

I never realized how complicated photo shoots are!

1 VOCABULARY Clothing repair

A Look at the clothing facts. What do you do with old clothes? Do you repair them? Recycle them? Throw them away?

OUR CLOTHING BY THE NUMBERS

- It takes 700 gallons of water to make one cotton shirt.
- Clothes can take up to 40 years to decompose.*
- Shoes can take up to 1,000 years to decompose.

- 95% of clothing can be recycled.
- 70% of people in the world wear used clothing.

*be slowly destroyed by a natural process; break down

B ▶07-08 Read the advertisement. Then listen and repeat the vocabulary words.

Do your clothes need repair?

If it's too loose, we can **take** it **in**.

If it's too tight, we can **let** it **out**.

We can:

repair holes　　replace zippers　　hem pants　　lengthen sleeves　　do other sewing　　and **dry clean**!

C PAIRS Talk about the tailor's services. Are they difficult to do? Would you do these things yourself or pay someone else to do them?

A: I think hemming pants is easy. I've done it myself, but I've never paid for it.
B: I don't know how to replace a zipper. I would pay someone to do it, or ask my aunt.

2 GRAMMAR Passive causatives

Use passive causatives to talk about having things done by other people.

	Get / have	Subject	Participle	
They need to	**get**	the light	fixed.	
Did you	**get**	your suit	dry cleaned?	
I hope the models	**have**	their makeup	done	on time.
Note: Causatives *get* and *have* mean the same thing.				

>> FOR PRACTICE, GO TO PAGE 144

3 CONVERSATION SKILL

A ▶07-09 Read the conversation skill. Listen. Notice how the speakers accept compliments.

1. A: Did you get your hair cut? It looks great!
   B: That's so nice. Thank you.
2. A: You're an excellent artist.
   B: Thanks! That's kind of you to say.

B Complete the compliments. Then take turns saying them to a partner and accepting them. Use the language from the conversation skill box.

1. You're an excellent _____ .
2. Where did you buy that _____ ? It's really nice.
3. You're very _____ .

4 CONVERSATION

A ▶07-10 Listen or watch. What are they talking about?

a. what happened at the photo shoot
b. why the photo shoot is happening Wednesday
c. where they are going to find different models

B ▶07-11 Listen or watch again. Answer the questions.

1. What compliment does Ed give to Leti?
2. What's the problem with the room?
3. What are Ed and Leti going to do later?

Do you think Leti is upset about things not being ready for the photo shoot? Have you ever had a problem because someone wasn't prepared? How did you react?

C ▶07-12 FOCUS ON LANGUAGE Listen. Complete the conversation.

Leti: Let's see … Mindy's skirt is too loose, so we need to _____ . John spilled something on his jacket, so we need to _____ . Marta broke the zipper on her pants, so we need to _____ .

Ed: Oh, boy.

5 TRY IT YOURSELF

A THINK Make a list of four clothing items (real or imaginary) that you want to have fixed.

B ROLE PLAY Student A: You're the customer. Explain to the tailor what the problem is and what you want done. Student B: You're the tailor. Tell the customer whether you can make the repair and how much it will cost.

A: *I need to get these pants hemmed.*
B: *I can do that. It will be $10.*

C ANALYZE Share the clothing problems with the class. Talk about whether you would really have the items repaired, repair them yourself, or throw them out and why.

■ I CAN TALK ABOUT CLOTHING REPAIRS.

ED MILLER

@EdM

First big project after my promotion.
I'm so nervous. Maybe I should wear
a superhero T-shirt!

1 BEFORE YOU LISTEN

A ▶07-13 VOCABULARY Listen.
Then listen and repeat.

> **confident:** believing you can do something well and without feeling nervous
> **physically:** related to your body, not your mind
> **an attitude:** the way you think or feel about something
> **a negotiator:** someone who negotiates
> **negotiate:** to talk about something in order to get an agreement
> **traditional:** based on ideas and ways of doing things that have existed for a long time
> **a social life:** the time you spend enjoying yourself with friends
> **socialize:** to spend time with people for fun

B Complete the sentences with the words in 1A. Use each word only once.

1. When you buy a new car, you need to _____ to get a good deal.
2. It's _____ in many countries for businesspeople to wear dark-colored suits.
3. I like to _____ with my co-workers at a restaurant after work.
4. Of course your job is important, but your _____ is important, too.
5. A good athlete must be _____ strong.
6. My boss is an excellent _____ . He always gets the best deals.
7. It's easier to do a good job if you feel _____ .
8. Carol is always smiling and never gets upset at work. She has a great _____ .

C PAIRS Discuss the questions.

1. Are you a good negotiator? How do you feel when you have to negotiate something?
2. Do you think you have a good balance between your social life and work or school? Why?
3. Where do you feel the most confident (for example, at work, when you are socializing)? Why?
4. What day of the week do you socialize the most? Why?
5. Would you describe your clothing style as traditional? Why or why not?
6. Do you think you have a good attitude toward school? Explain.

2 GRAMMAR *Would rather (than)*

Use *would rather (than)* to talk about preferences.

	Would	*Rather*	**Base verb**		
I	**would**	**rather**	be	comfortable	(than fashionable).
He	**would**	**rather**	stay	home	(than go out).
You	**would**	**rather not**	wear	a suit	(than wear one).

Note: In speaking and informal writing, we usually use contractions with subject pronouns and *would. I'd rather wear a T-shirt.*

>> FOR PRACTICE, GO TO PAGE 145

3 LISTENING

A ▶07-14 Listen or watch. What is the speaker's main idea?

   a. It's important to dress formally at work.

   b. Choose the right clothing for the right situation.

   c. You'll feel more confident if you wear a suit.

B ▶07-15 Read the Listening Skill. Listen or watch again. Complete the sentences giving the speaker's opinions.

   1. _____ , your clothing can be the key to feeling good, making a good impression on others, and being successful.

   2. So _____ that if you need to negotiate—for example, if you're buying a car—dress formally.

Adriana Lopez | TSW Global Speaker Program
Unit 7: Clothing, attitude, and success

> **LISTENING SKILL Listen for opinions**
>
> Sometimes speakers use expressions like these to make it clear that they are giving an opinion:
> *I think*   *In my opinion*
> *If you ask me*   *I would say*
> Listen for these expressions to identify the speaker's opinion.

C ▶07-16 Listen or watch again. Complete the sentences with the words in the box.

confident	formally	friendly	red	sneakers

   1. People who wear superhero shirts feel more _____ .

   2. Athletes wearing _____ are able to lift heavier weights.

   3. People who dressed _____ did better on tests of their thinking.

   4. People thought a professor wearing red _____ was more intelligent.

   5. Wearing business clothes can make people seem less _____ .

D VOCABULARY EXPANSION Read the sentences from the talk. What do the underlined expressions mean?

   1. Studies have shown that when people dress in business clothing, they do better on tests. Basically, when you dress more formally, your mind is <u>sharper</u>.

   2. When they saw pictures of a university professor wearing red sneakers, they thought he was more <u>competent</u> and a better teacher than a professor in traditional dress shoes.

   3. Some offices have "casual Fridays," where people dress informally at work once a week. That may not be <u>ideal</u> for Friday negotiations, but it's great for creating a friendly workplace.

E PAIRS Compare your answers in 3D.

4 DISCUSSION

A THINK What clothes make you feel the most confident in different social situations? Write the clothing items in the chart.

A fancy party	A movie night with friends	A dinner with co-workers

B DISCUSS In small groups, talk about your ideas in 4A.

I have a black dress and high heels that I like to wear to parties. I might wear the same thing to dinner with co-workers. I'd rather be too formal than too casual.

C COMPARE As a class, discuss the clothes that people like to wear in each situation. Are they the same or different? Why?

☐ I CAN DISCUSS FASHION AND ATTITUDE.

ED MILLER
@EdM

Just read an article about a fashion designer. Her job is pretty great in some ways, but I wouldn't want to do it.

1 BEFORE YOU READ

A   **PAIRS**   What makes a job interesting? Make a list of three ideas and share them.

I think a job is interesting if you meet new people …

B   ▶07-17 **VOCABULARY**   Listen. Then listen and repeat. Do you know these words?

a bridal gown   fabric   a ritual   specialize (in)   decorative   a rough sketch   a fitting room

>> FOR DEFINITIONS AND PRACTICE, GO TO PAGE 145

2 READ

A   **PREVIEW**   Look at the title and the photograph. How do you think she spends her day?

B   ▶07-18 Read and listen to the article. Was your prediction correct?

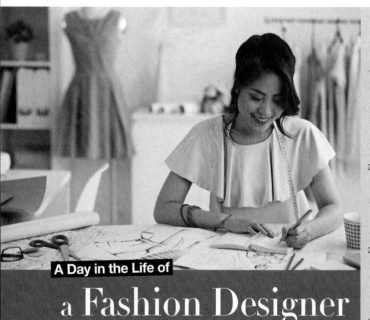

A Day in the Life of

a Fashion Designer

Clarissa Chen grew up in Hong Kong, the child of a talented dressmaker and a businessman, and she absorbed both of her parents' interests. After receiving her master's degree in fashion design in
5   London, she worked for a design house for a few years but soon decided that she wanted to open a business of her own. Now she owns a shop in London where women go to have bridal gowns and other special-event dresses designed and
10   made. We asked Clarissa what a day is like for someone with such an unusual profession.

8:00 AM I start the day at my desk, drinking coffee and going through my email. Then I wander through the shop to make sure that everything is ready for the day. I look over the fabric room
15   and check the sewing machines—it's a kind of starting-the-day ritual for me.

9:00 The three tailors come in. They all operate the sewing machines, but I have one tailor who specializes in hand sewing, and she does most of the decorative needlework on the dresses.

20   **9:30** My front desk manager, Kayla, comes in. She opens the shop and takes care of fabric orders and, most importantly, answers the phone. When they schedule an appointment, the clients tell Kayla about what they want and how soon they'll need it. This helps me prepare for meeting them.

25   **10:00** My first client comes into my office, and we talk about the style, color, and fabric for her dress. I really enjoy this process. Helping clients turn their ideas into a design is the most creative part of my job. I make a rough sketch, and then we go into the fitting room and I take measurements. I usually see two or three
30   clients in the morning.

12:00 PM The shop closes, and everyone goes to lunch. I eat at my desk and talk to clients.

1:00 I spend an hour or two sewing after lunch every day. It was my love of sewing that got me into this profession in the first
35   place, so I make sure I still make time for it.

3:00 In the afternoon, I see three or four more clients. Then Kayla and I work on the calendar to arrange work schedules for the next week.

6:00 Kayla closes up the shop and she and the tailors go home.

7:30 I go home, eat dinner, watch a little TV, and go to bed. I'm
40   tired after a long day, but I spend my time being creative, making beautiful things, and working with people. I wouldn't trade this life for anything!

3 CHECK YOUR UNDERSTANDING

A Read the article again. Which statement describes Clarissa's life?

   a. She works long days but loves her work.

   b. Her work is easy but not very interesting.

   c. She likes her work but wishes she had more free time.

B Circle the correct answers, according to the article.

   1. How many clients does Clarissa see every day?

      a. two to four

      b. three to five

      c. five to seven

   2. What does Kayla do?

      a. She meets with clients, helps the tailors, and does hand sewing.

      b. She takes care of the email and checks the sewing machines.

      c. She orders fabric, arranges schedules, and answers the phone.

   3. Which things does Clarissa really enjoy?

      a. sewing and working with clients to design dresses

      b. taking measurements and arranging the work schedule

      c. looking over the fabric room and talking to clients on the phone

C CLOSE READING Reread lines 1–11. Then circle the correct answers.

   1. What does *she absorbed both of her parents' interests* mean?

      a. She enjoyed all of her parents' hobbies.

      b. She became interested in dressmaking and business.

      c. Her parents spent a lot of time with her when she was a child.

   2. What part of Clarissa's career path was probably influenced by her father?

      a. receiving a master's degree in fashion design

      b. working for a design house for a few years

      c. deciding to open a business of her own

D Read the Reading Skill. Go back to the article and underline the reasons that Clarissa Chen likes working with clients, makes time for sewing, and wouldn't trade her life for anything.

> **READING SKILL** Identify reasons
>
> Writers often use words such as *so* and *because* to connect reasons with the ideas they support. However, sometimes the relationship between two ideas is very clear and the reader is expected to make the connection without one of these words.

E PAIRS What is the article about? Summarize the most important ideas. Use your own words.

The article is about how a fashion designer spends her day. She ...

How do people become fashion designers?

4 MAKE IT PERSONAL

A If you had a job like Clarissa Chen's, what would you like about it? What wouldn't you like about it? Take notes in the chart.

Pros	Cons

B PAIRS Compare your ideas in 4A.

One good thing about her job is that she is her own boss, but ...

■ I CAN READ ABOUT A FASHION DESIGNER.

ED MILLER
@EdM

Shopping for new work clothes! What kind of outfit says "professional, but still cool"?

1 BEFORE YOU WRITE

A How would you describe your personal clothing style? Do you think having a personal style is important?

B Read the responses to a question online. Who is Mateo's style idol? Who is Kristen's?

TODAY'S STYLE: WHO'S YOUR STYLE IDOL?

Have you heard the saying "The clothes make the man"? Personal style is important. What we wear can tell the world a lot about who we are, what we think, and what is important to us. So we asked our readers: Who is your style idol—the person whose clothing style you like best? Here are some of their responses:

Mateo Diaz, 30

Without a doubt, my personal style idol is my co-worker, Luis. Luis has a good job, but he is not rich and can't afford extremely expensive clothes. However, he always looks like he stepped out of a magazine! At work, he always looks professional, but he still looks cool and individual, like a classic movie star. For example, he'll wear a nice pair of dark jeans, a dark blue suit jacket, and a white shirt. Each of these items is kind of plain, but they are always perfectly tailored. And he always wears his clothes with confidence, which, as far as I'm concerned, is the most important thing.

Kristen Walters, 28

Personal style is so important in today's world, and in my mind, clothing is a way to communicate your personality. My sister, Violet, is a great communicator! She has a fun, vintage style. She shops at vintage clothing stores and always finds something colorful and unique. My favorite outfit of hers is a gold jacket that she wears with a bright shirt and hat. Her style tells the world that she is a creative and friendly person. I love that!

C Read the responses again. Complete the chart with information from the responses.

Person	Style	Examples	Why he or she likes it

2 FOCUS ON WRITING

Read the Writing Skill. Then reread the text in 1B. Circle the phrases that show that the writer is expressing his or her opinion and underline the opinion he or she is giving.

3 PLAN YOUR WRITING

A Think of someone you know or a celebrity who has a personal style that you really like. Complete the chart with information about this person's style.

Person	Style	Examples	Why I like it

B PAIRS Talk about your ideas. Suggest ways your partner can improve or add to his or her ideas.

Can you give another example ...

4 WRITE

Write a response to the question "Who's your style idol?" Make sure you use phrases that make it clear that you are giving your opinion. Use the responses in 1B as a model.

Drafting tip

Don't be afraid of making mistakes in your first draft. Let your ideas come out, and don't worry too much about spelling and grammar. You can always fix your mistakes later.

5 REVISE YOUR WRITING

A PAIRS Exchange and read each other's responses.

1. Underline the type of style. Is it clear what it is?
2. Put a check mark (✔) next to examples of the style. Can you clearly imagine what the person wears?
3. Circle any words or phrases that show the writer is expressing an opinion.

B PAIRS Can your partner improve his or her response? Make suggestions.

6 PROOFREAD

Read your response again. Check your

- spelling
- punctuation
- capitalization

I CAN WRITE ABOUT PERSONAL STYLE.

PUT IT TOGETHER

1 PRESENTATION PROJECT

▶ **A** ▶07-19 Listen or watch. What is the topic of the presentation?

_____

▶ **B** ▶07-20 Listen or watch again. Answer the questions.

1. What do the people in Misaki's examples wear?
   Person 1: _____
   Person 2: _____
2. Do the people's clothes match reality? Why or why not?
   Person 1: _____
   Person 2: _____

C Read the Presentation Skill. What kind of information should you write on note cards?

D Make your own presentation.

Step 1 Brainstorm examples of how the meaning of the expression "Don't judge a book by its cover" can be applied to someone's clothing.

Step 2 Prepare a two-minute presentation about this idea using your examples. Bring an item or picture that is related to your examples.

> ### PRESENTATION SKILL
>
> **Use notes**
> To remember what you want to say and the order you want to say it in, write notes on note cards. Write only key words—not sentences—so you don't just read from the cards.

Step 3 Give your presentation to the class. Use notes to help you remember what to say. Answer questions and get feedback.

> How did you do? Complete the self-evaluation on page 165.

2 REFLECT AND PLAN

A Look back through the unit. Check (✓) the things you learned. Highlight the things you need to learn.

Speaking objectives
- ☐ Talk about people's clothes
- ☐ Talk about clothing repairs
- ☐ Discuss fashion and attitude

Vocabulary
- ☐ Verbs related to clothing
- ☐ Adjectives related to clothing
- ☐ Clothing repair

Conversation
- ☐ Accept compliments

Pronunciation
- ☐ Emphatic stress

Listening
- ☐ Listen for opinions

Grammar
- ☐ Reduced defining relative clauses
- ☐ Passive causatives
- ☐ _Would rather (than)_

Reading
- ☐ Identify reasons

Writing
- ☐ Express opinions

B What will you do to learn the things you highlighted? For example, use your app, review your Student Book, or do other practice. Make a plan.

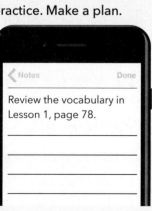

‹ Notes   Done

Review the vocabulary in Lesson 1, page 78.

_____
_____
_____

8 DO I NEED TO INSTALL SOMETHING?

LEARNING GOALS

In this unit, you
- ⊘ talk about regrets
- ⊘ describe using a computer
- ⊘ discuss social media and friendship
- ⊘ read about a high-tech city
- ⊘ write about a new technology

GET STARTED

A Read the unit title and the learning goals.

B Look at the photo. What's going on?

C Now read Paula's message. What kind of week is Paula having?

PAULA FLOREZ
@PaulaF

Ever feel like your computer is taking up all of your time? I'm having one of those weeks. 😕

PAULA FLOREZ
@PaulaF

I'm not bad with technology, but sometimes I think I should learn more.

1 VOCABULARY Technology

A ▶08-01 Read the website. Then listen and repeat the vocabulary words.

TECHNOLOGY INSTITUTE

Learn the latest **software**: Graphic design, video editing, and more! We have the latest **versions** of all of the **programs** you're interested in.

Coding classes: Learn how to **code** and then build your own **apps**!

Basic Instruction: Learn how to protect your computer from **viruses** and how to set up your home **network.**

More interested in **hardware**? We have classes in computer repair!

code

software

apps (applications)

a virus

a network

hardware

B Complete the sentences with the words in 1A.

1. Apps and programs are kinds of _____ . They tell a computer what to do.
2. The computer _____ is made of plastic and metal.
3. _____ is short for "application." It's a _____ designed to do a specific thing, like tell you the weather.
4. Computers in an office or in a home are usually connected by a private _____ .
5. If you want to program a computer, you need to learn how to _____ . There are a lot of schools that offer classes in _____ .
6. Technology is changing all the time, so new _____ of software come out frequently.
7. _____ can cause a lot of damage to computer software.

C PAIRS Discuss the questions.

1. What apps do you use the most?
2. Are you interested in learning how to code? In computer hardware?
3. How do you protect your computer from viruses?

2 GRAMMAR Wish / If only to express regrets

Use *I wish / If only* + past perfect to describe regrets you have about things you did or didn't do in the past.

Subject	*Wish*	Subject	Past perfect	
I	wish	I	had paid attention	to the teacher.
She	wishes	she	hadn't missed	the class.

If only	Subject	Past perfect	
If only	I	had studied	coding.
If only	we	had arrived	earlier.

>> FOR PRACTICE, GO TO PAGE 146

3 PRONUNCIATION

(A) ▶08-02 Read and listen to the pronunciation note.

(B) ▶08-03 Listen. Notice how the auxiliary verb *had* is pronounced. Then listen again and repeat.

If only I'<u>d</u> paid more attention.
If only Jasper <u>had</u> studied harder.
Ana wishes she'<u>d</u> taken the coding class.
I wish the app <u>had</u> worked better.
If only they <u>hadn't</u> been late.

> ### Contractions of the auxiliary *had*
>
> In the past perfect, *had* is usually contracted after pronouns: *I'd, you'd, he'd, she'd, we'd, they'd*. The /d/ is short. Do not pause or add a vowel after the contraction.
>
> After nouns, *had* may be reduced to /ɪd/ and linked closely to the words around it:
> *I wish Peter /ɪd/ seen it.*
>
> The negative past perfect auxiliary *hadn't* is stressed: *I hàdn't seen the movie.*

(C) ▶08-04 Listen. If you hear the past perfect auxiliary verb (*'d, had, hadn't*), write it in the blank.

1. a. We _____ studied coding.
   b. We _____ studied coding.
2. a. I wish I _____ sent that email.
   b. I wish I _____ sent that email.
3. a. Ed _____ built his own app.
   b. Ed _____ built his own app.
4. a. He _____ heard the news.
   b. He _____ heard the news.

4 CONVERSATION

(A) ▶08-05 Listen or watch. What are they talking about?
a. Ahmet's school days
b. Paula's regrets
c. their experiences at work

(B) ▶08-06 Listen or watch again. Answer the questions.
1. What does Ahmet like about his job?
2. What does Ahmet say about learning to use the design software?
3. What advice does Ahmet give Paula?

> Do you agree with Ahmet's advice? Why or why not?

(C) ▶08-07 FOCUS ON LANGUAGE Listen. Complete the conversation.

Paula:	I wish _____ more about computers when I was in school. I don't know anything except for, you know, basic office programs.
Ahmet:	Really?
Paula:	Yeah. A lot of my friends were into technology, but I was never really interested. Now they're all working as programmers at tech companies and making a lot of money. And I think to myself, "If only _____ to code!"

5 TRY IT YOURSELF

(A) PAIRS Brainstorm a list of problems you or someone you know has with technology.

(B) ROLE PLAY Explain the problems. Talk about something you wish you or the other person had done to avoid them.
I don't know how to fix my computer. I wish I'd taken a basic repair class.

(C) ANALYZE Tell your problems and regrets to the class. Discuss which problems are the easiest and most difficult to solve.

■ I CAN TALK ABOUT REGRETS.

LESSON 2 DESCRIBE USING A COMPUTER

PAULA FLOREZ
@PaulaF

I have to learn some new software at work. I hope it's not too complicated!

1 VOCABULARY Using software

A ▶08-08 Read the instructions. Then listen and repeat the vocabulary words.

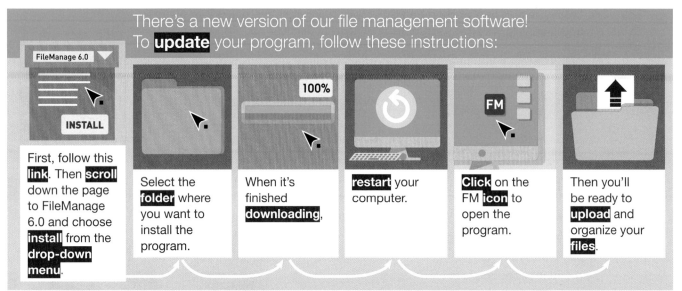

There's a new version of our file management software!
To **update** your program, follow these instructions:

FileManage 6.0

INSTALL

First, follow this **link**. Then **scroll** down the page to FileManage 6.0 and choose **install** from the **drop-down menu**.

Select the **folder** where you want to install the program.

100%

When it's finished **downloading**,

restart your computer.

FM

Click on the FM **icon** to open the program.

Then you'll be ready to **upload** and organize your **files**.

B Write the words in the chart.

Things on a computer	Things you do on a computer

C PAIRS Think about a program or an app you use. Explain to your partner how to get it and how to use it. Use words in 1A.

I use an app to see the basketball scores. You click on the icon to open it, and then you click on a drop-down menu and choose the game you want to check.

2 GRAMMAR Showing purpose

Use (*in order*) *to* + base verb and *for* + noun or gerund to show purpose.

	In order	*To*	**Base verb**	
You have to click on the link	(in order)	to	update	your software.
We use this program			organize	our files.

	For	**Noun or gerund**	
Click on this link	for	information about the new software.	
We use this program		managing files.	

>> FOR PRACTICE, GO TO PAGE 147

3 CONVERSATION SKILL

A ▶08-09 Read the conversation skill. Listen. Notice how the speakers respond to gratitude.

1. A: Thank you so much!
   B: It's not a problem—glad to help.
2. A: I really appreciate this.
   B: My pleasure.

B Walk around. Talk to five people. Take turns expressing gratitude and responding.

4 CONVERSATION

A ▶08-10 Listen or watch. Who figures out how to solve the problem?

B ▶08-11 Listen or watch again. Answer the questions.

1. What is Paula trying to do?
2. What does Marcos suggest she do to update her computer?
3. Why doesn't Marcos know a lot about file management programs?

> Why is Paula happy at the end of the conversation? When you have computer problems, do you try to figure them out yourself or ask for help? Why?

C ▶08-12 FOCUS ON LANGUAGE Listen. Complete the conversation.

Marcos: Now open this _____ , and scroll down to Carla's name.

Paula: Yeah, I got that. But when I try to add the file, nothing happens.

Marcos: Oh. Huh. That should work.

Paula: Wait a second, what's this icon? Oh! I get it. _____ in her folder, I need to click *here* and then choose "upload file" from the drop-down menu.

5 TRY IT YOURSELF

A THINK Add two more ideas to the list of technology tasks.

- upload a new profile picture
- organize files on your computer
- _____
- _____

B PAIRS Choose a task from 5A. Explain how to perform the task. Use *(in order) to* + base verb or *for* + noun / gerund to show the purpose of each step.

First, go to the photos on your phone to find a picture you like. Open your social media app and click on your profile in order to see the "Edit Profile" button.

C COMPARE Choose one partner's task and say the instructions for the class. See if everyone agrees about the steps.

I CAN DESCRIBE USING A COMPUTER.

PAULA FLOREZ

@PaulaF

Did you know most people have about 15 close friends?

1 BEFORE YOU LISTEN

A Look at the chart. How does your time on social media sites compare to the averages in these countries?

Hours Spent on Social Media Every Day

Country	Hours
Philippines	(3.7)
Mexico	(3.2)
Turkey	(2.5)
China	(1.5)
Japan	(0.3)

0.0 0.5 1.0 1.5 2.0 2.5 3.0 3.5 4.0

B ▶08-13 VOCABULARY Listen. Then listen and repeat. Do you know these words?

> **offend**: to make someone angry or upset
> **stay in touch**: to continue to communicate with someone who does not live near you
> **an anthropologist**: someone who studies people
> **consider**: to have an opinion about something
> **lose touch**: to not stay in touch
> **cut off**: to end a connection with someone or something
> **face-to-face**: in person, not over the phone or internet

C ▶08-14 Listen to the story. Then complete the sentences. Use words in 1B in your answers. Use correct verb tenses.

1. Carlos is a(n) _____ .
2. When Teruko moved back to Japan, she and Carlos _____ .
3. When Teruko didn't send him a birthday message, Carlos was _____ .
4. This year, they have _____ .
5. Carlos _____ Teruko to be a wonderful person and friend.
6. Next year, they plan to meet _____ .

2 GRAMMAR *Even* to emphasize a point

Use *even* or *not even* to stress an idea or emphasize a point. In most cases, place *even* between the subject and the main verb or after the auxiliary verb.

Subject	Auxiliary verb	(Not) even	Main verb	
Time spent online	can	**even**	damage	your relationships.
You	may	**not even**	be spending	enough time with your husband or wife.

Place *even* after the verb *be* when it is the main verb.

There **is**		**even**	a study about that.	

You can sometimes place *even* before words, phrases, and clauses you want to emphasize.

He remembers friends' birthdays,		**even**	those he doesn't see very often.	

>> FOR PRACTICE, GO TO PAGE 148

3 LISTENING

A ▶08-15 Listen or watch. Which statement matches the speaker's point of view?

   a. People feel better when they have a lot of friends on social media.

   b. Most friendships are not as close anymore because of social media.

   c. Social media is good for casual friendships but not for close friendships.

B ▶08-16 Read the Listening Skill. Listen or watch again. Complete the sentences referring to sources.

   1. _____ , we don't realize how important human touch is to us.

   2. _____ that people who spend a lot of time online are lonelier than those who spend less.

> **TSW MEDIA**
>
> Kendrick Scott | TSW Global Speaker Program
> **Unit 8: Is social media ruining your friendships?**

> **LISTENING SKILL** Listen for sources
>
> Speakers often refer to sources, either by name or in general, using expressions like these:
> *According to (Smith), …*
> *Psychologists say …*
> *Scientists have found …*
> *Studies have shown …*
> *In a 1990 study, (Jones) found …*

C ▶08-17 Listen or watch again. Complete the sentences with the words in the box.

casual	deeper	shared	close
damaged	good		

   1. Most people have about 15 _____ friends and about 50 _____ friends.

   2. Because of social media, we don't lose touch with our _____ friends anymore.

   3. Social media doesn't make your close friendships _____ .

   4. Face-to-face friendships give people _____ experiences.

   5. Important relationships can be _____ by too much time spent online.

D VOCABULARY EXPANSION Read the sentences. What do the underlined expressions mean?

   1. Recently, my friend Anita <u>unfriended</u> 200 people on social media. She just deleted them from her contacts list.

   2. The outer group—around 100 people <u>or so</u>—are casual friends.

   3. Your friend patting you on the back when you're <u>down</u> can comfort you in a way that no on-screen conversation can.

E PAIRS Compare your answers in 3D.

4 DISCUSSION

A THINK Make a list of how social media affects your friendships in good and bad ways.

keep in touch with old friends
sometimes argue with friends online

B DISCUSS Share your ideas in small groups and decide if you would like to have fewer online friends or spend less or more time on social media.

A: Do you think you spend too much time on social media?
B: No, I think I spend about the right amount of time online—I still have lots of time to see friends face-to-face.

C COMPARE How many people in the class feel that social media sometimes has a negative effect on their friendships? How many don't?

   ■ I CAN DISCUSS SOCIAL MEDIA AND FRIENDSHIP.

PAULA FLOREZ
@PaulaF

I just read an article about a new high-tech city. Sounds interesting, but I'm not sure I'd want to live there.

1 BEFORE YOU READ

A PAIRS What are some problems of living in a city? How can city planners make them better?

One problem of living in a city is …

B ▶08-18 VOCABULARY Listen. Then listen and repeat. Do you know these words?

a structure	efficient	modular	revolutionary	a resident
an alternative	a pedestrian	a sensor	monitor	unique

>> FOR DEFINITIONS AND PRACTICE, GO TO PAGE 148

2 READ

A PREVIEW Look at the title and the picture. What do you think the "city of tomorrow" is like?

B ▶08-19 Read and listen to the article. Were your predictions correct?

City of Tomorrow

Greenville is not a place you want to walk at night. Few people live there, nobody shops there, and it's full of empty apartment buildings and factories. But if
5 technology giant CITtech gets its way, all of that will be changing very soon.

The first part of CITtech's plan is to replace most of the existing structures with new housing, commercial buildings, and streets, and to build a revolutionary new
10 transportation system.

As you would expect, all of the new buildings will be high tech and energy efficient. They will also be modular. That means that each building will be constructed from pre-made sections, similar to building blocks. This
15 revolutionary approach means that if more space is needed, it will be easy to add another room.

The city's residents will share a large group of self-driving vehicles, so fewer people will have to own their own cars. And, as a cheaper alternative to the cars, driverless buses
20 will run on all of the main streets. There will also be a large network of tunnels beneath the city used by robots to remove and sort trash and deliver mail and packages. This will keep service and delivery vehicles off the city streets, making traffic lighter. CITtech believes that the efficient
25 traffic system will allow the streets to be narrower and the sidewalks wider, making the city better for pedestrians.

Creating an efficient city requires more than buildings and roads. The real key to Greenville's success will be the sensors built into every structure. These sensors will
30 gather data that can be used to improve services. For example, sensors will monitor how much waste people are producing, and how much water and electricity they use, which means that the city will always know when and where more service is needed. For example, the trash
35 collectors won't waste time picking up empty bins and will go where the most trash is found. For residents, this will mean no waiting for services.

>>

> The streets and sidewalks will also have sensors and cameras that will monitor car and pedestrian traffic. Imagine that a large group of people gathers at a bus stop. That information will be gathered
40 by the system so additional buses can be added. And when the traffic sensors detect heavy traffic, the city's driverless cars will automatically take a different route.

A lot of cities are employing smart technologies these days, but Greenville will be unique because of its efficient traffic system and the large amount of data about the residents. This plan is designed for growth, and there's no doubt that CITtech will come up with more exciting ideas for improving the
45 lives of residents. Keep your eye on Greenville—you may want to move there pretty soon.

3 CHECK YOUR UNDERSTANDING

A Read the article again. What is the writer's opinion of Greenville?
   a. The plan is interesting, but it could be very expensive.
   b. The new ideas should be tested before people begin living there.
   c. The technology will make its residents' lives easier and better.

B Answer the questions according to the article.
   1. Who created the plan for Greenville? _____
   2. Why does the writer think modular buildings are revolutionary? _____
   3. How will the sensors help transportation in the city? _____

C CLOSE READING Reread lines 20-24. Then circle the correct answers.
   1. In line 22, what does *This* refer to?
      a. the network of tunnels
      b. the city
      c. the entire first sentence
   2. What will make traffic lighter?
      a. service and delivery vehicles being off the streets
      b. vehicles delivering mail and packages
      c. service vehicles removing and sorting trash

D Read the Reading Skill. Go back to the article and underline the adjectives that describe the plan for Greenville. Do you think the writer is biased?

> **READING SKILL** Recognize bias
>
> Writers often use adjectives to show how they feel about their topic. If a text contains a large number of either positive or negative adjectives, it may be a sign that the writer is biased. A biased writer is only looking at one side of an issue.

E PAIRS What is the article about? Summarize the most important ideas.

   The article is about the plans for a city called Greenville. It's going to have ...

What are the world's most high-tech cities?

4 MAKE IT PERSONAL

A If you were thinking about living in Greenville, what questions would have after reading this article? Write your questions about each topic in the chart.

Housing	Transportation	Data about residents	Other

B PAIRS Compare your questions in 4A with a partner. Do you think you'd want to live in a city like Greenville? Why or why not?

   I wouldn't want to live in a city like Greenville because ...

■ I CAN READ ABOUT A HIGH-TECH CITY.

PAULA FLOREZ
@PaulaF

I like to travel, but I think New York is far enough for me!

1 BEFORE YOU WRITE

A What new technology do you think will change the way people live or work in the future? Make a prediction.

B Read the website article about a possible future technology. What will people be able to do?

Space | Communication | Technology

FUTURE TECH

Do you wonder if Earth is big enough for our growing population? The world's cities are becoming more crowded every year. Having enough land and clean water for everyone on Earth could be a problem in the future, but the answer may be found on the moon or another planet, where humans could build new towns and cities. But how could we even get people to space? And how could humans travel through space quickly and inexpensively?

We've all been on an elevator inside of a building. You push a button and are taken to another floor. But how about if instead of choosing a floor when getting on an elevator, you could choose a planet? Many experts on the future think that one day, there will be a space elevator and it will transport people from Earth to the moon, and even to Mars.

How would this elevator work? Scientists are trying to create a 100,000-kilometer (62,137-mile) "ribbon" that could be attached to Earth and then extended and attached to the moon or another planet. Travelers will simply enter a car that can move up and down the ribbon, just like the elevators we all ride today. A space elevator would be much less expensive and could transport many more people than the rockets that have previously been used for space travel.

This elevator to the stars is probably at least 40 or 50 years away, but many scientists around the world are working on the technology right now. So get your suitcases ready!

2 FOCUS ON WRITING

A Read the Writing Skill. Underline the problem identified in the article.

B Read the article again. Complete the chart with information about the problem and the solution.

> **WRITING SKILL** Explain a problem and solution
>
> To explain a problem and solution, first, clearly state the problem and the reasons why it is a problem. Then explain the solution. Add details about why the solution would work and what the result of the solution would be.

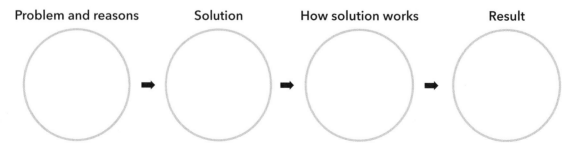

Problem and reasons ➡ Solution ➡ How solution works ➡ Result

3 PLAN YOUR WRITING

A Think of a problem today in travel, communication, or medicine. How could this problem be solved with technology? Complete the chart with information about the problem, the solution, and the result.

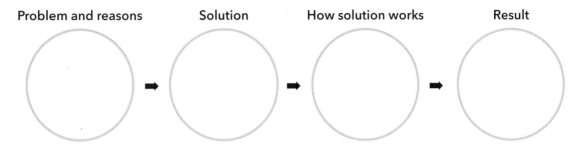

Problem and reasons → Solution → How solution works → Result

B PAIRS Talk about your ideas. Suggest ways your partner can improve or add to his or her ideas.

I like your solution, but I don't understand ...

4 WRITE

Write a description of a problem in the world today that could be solved with better technology in the future. Use the article in 1B as a model.

Writing tip

Know your audience. If you are writing for people who don't know a lot about technology, keep your explanations simple, and don't use too much special vocabulary.

5 REVISE YOUR WRITING

A PAIRS Exchange and read each other's descriptions of a problem and solution.

1. Underline the problem. Is it clear what it is?
2. Circle the solution.
3. Put a check mark (✔) next to how the solution works. Do you understand the explanation?
4. Can you understand how the result is related to the solution?

B PAIRS Can your partner improve his or her description? Make suggestions.

6 PROOFREAD

Read your article again. Check your

- spelling
- punctuation
- capitalization

PUT IT TOGETHER

1 PRESENTATION PROJECT

▶ **A** ▶08-20 Listen or watch. What is the topic of the presentation?

_____

▶ **B** ▶08-21 Listen or watch again. Answer the questions.

1. What are the names of the two apps Junio uses?
   App 1: _____
   App 2: _____

2. What do the apps do?
   App 1: _____
   App 2: _____

C Read the Presentation Skill. What kind of information can be presented with a graph or chart?

D Make your own presentation.

Step 1 Think about two or three of your favorite apps or websites that could be useful to your classmates.

Step 2 Prepare a two-minute presentation about those apps or sites. Make and bring a chart that is related to them.

Step 3 Give your presentation to the class. Answer questions and get feedback.

> ### PRESENTATION SKILL
>
> **Use charts**
> Presenting facts in a graph or chart makes the information easier to understand. Charts can also help highlight important facts in your presentation.

How did you do? Complete the self-evaluation on page 165.

2 REFLECT AND PLAN

A Look back through the unit. Check (✓) the things you learned. Highlight the things you need to learn.

Speaking objectives
- ☐ Talk about regrets
- ☐ Describe using a computer
- ☐ Discuss social media and friendship

Vocabulary
- ☐ Technology
- ☐ Using software

Conversation
- ☐ Respond to gratitude

Pronunciation
- ☐ Contractions of the auxiliary *had*

Listening
- ☐ Listen for sources

Grammar
- ☐ *Wish / If only* to express regrets
- ☐ Showing purpose
- ☐ *Even* to emphasize a point

Reading
- ☐ Recognize bias

Writing
- ☐ Explain a problem and solution

B What will you do to learn the things you highlighted? For example, use your app, review your Student Book, or do other practice. Make a plan.

‹ Notes   Done

Review the vocabulary in Lesson 2, page 92.

_____
_____
_____
_____

ARE YOU READY TO WALK AWAY?

LEARNING GOALS

In this unit, you
- ⊘ talk about a past negotiation
- ⊘ negotiate a deal
- ⊘ discuss negotiation skills
- ⊘ read about negotiating styles
- ⊘ write about a conflict

GET STARTED

A Read the unit title and the learning goals.

B Look at the photo. What's going on?

C Now read Lan's message. What is different about her?

LAN PHAM
@LanP

A lot of people hate negotiating, but I enjoy it. And I'm pretty good at it!

LAN PHAM
@LanP
Successful negotiations are so satisfying! ☺

 1 VOCABULARY People at a conference

A ▶09-01 Listen. Then listen and repeat.

maintenance staff

a security officer

a greeter

wait staff

a caterer

a presenter

a supervisor

a technical (tech) support team

B ▶09-02 Listen. Who is speaking? Circle the correct answers.

1. a. supervisor   b. wait staff   c. tech support team
2. a. presenter   b. caterer   c. security officer
3. a. greeter   b. wait staff   c. maintenance staff
4. a. supervisor   b. greeter   c. tech support team
5. a. caterer   b. maintenance staff   c. greeter
6. a. tech support team   b. wait staff   c. security officer
7. a. greeter   b. maintenance staff   c. supervisor
8. a. security officer   b. caterer   c. presenter

C PAIRS Discuss the jobs in 1A. Which are the most interesting? Which job would you like the most? The least?

2 GRAMMAR Causative verbs: *get*, *have*, and *make*

Use causative verbs to talk about causing someone to do something.
Use *get* to talk about persuading someone to do something.

Subject	Get	Person	Infinitive verb	
I	**got**	the caterer	to add	a vegetarian dish.
She	**will get**	the presenter	to start	a little later.

Use *have* to talk about a person doing something because you requested it.
Use *make* to talk about forcing or requiring someone to do something.

Subject	Have / make	Person	Base verb	
I	**had**	the greeter	stand	at the door.
I	**can't make**	them	give	us a discount.

>> FOR PRACTICE, GO TO PAGE 149

3 CONVERSATION SKILL

A ▶09-03 Read the conversation skill. Listen. Notice how the speakers end the phone call.

A: Thanks for calling. It was great talking to you.
B: You, too. Let's talk again soon.
A: Yes, definitely.
B: Bye-bye.

> **End a phone call**
>
> Before you say "good-bye," end a phone call politely by using expressions like these:
> *Thank you for calling.*
> *It was great talking to you.*
> *Let's talk again soon.*
> *I'll talk to you Friday.*

B Complete the sentences. Then practice the conversation with a partner.

A: I have to get going. I'll _____ Monday, OK?
B: Sounds good! Thank you _____ .

A: Of course! Goodbye.
B: Bye.

4 CONVERSATION

A ▶09-04 Listen or watch. What are they talking about?

a. Lan's first big negotiation
b. Lan's thoughts on why the hotel is difficult to work with
c. Lan's preparations for a big meeting

B ▶09-05 Listen or watch again. Answer the questions.

1. According to Leti, why do the managers like Lan?
2. What does the hotel provide for the conference?
3. Why did Leti like the caterers last year?

> How does Lan feel about negotiating? Do you like to negotiate? Why or why not?

C ▶09-06 FOCUS ON LANGUAGE Listen. Complete the conversation.

Lan:	I just _____ us a big discount on the conference rooms.
Leti:	Good work! Is this for the sales meeting?
Lan:	Yep. It's going to be huge this year–we've got about 300 people coming.
Leti:	Wow! That's a lot of people.
Lan:	Which is why I also _____ us the main ballroom a day early.

5 TRY IT YOURSELF

A THINK Think about a time you negotiated with someone at work or in your personal life. Write your ideas in the chart.

Who did you negotiate with?	
What did you get the person to do?	
How did the person react?	

B PAIRS Tell your partner about the situation.

A: I negotiated with my boss last month. I got him to give me an extra day off.
B: How did you do that?
A: I offered to help on a big project. He needed help, and I really wanted a day off!

C EVALUATE Decide who had the most difficult negotiation in the class.

☐ **I CAN TALK ABOUT A PAST NEGOTIATION.**

1 VOCABULARY Verbs for negotiating

LAN PHAM
@LanP

In any negotiation, it's important to know what you want and what you will not accept.

A ▶09-07 Listen. Then listen and repeat.

It's a deal!
make an agreement

sign a contract

cancel an agreement

Five hundred sounds good. It's yours!
accept an offer

Sorry, the salary isn't high enough.
reject an offer

You should try this on.
make a suggestion

I can work for $70 an hour, $65 an hour $60 an hour
offer a lower rate

I'm finished!
walk away

B Write the words from 1A in the correct categories.

The negotiation is going well	The negotiation is going badly

C PAIRS Talk about the verbs in 1A. What are some situations where people accept / reject an offer? Make / cancel an agreement? Sign a contract / walk away?

People accept job offers when they like the job.

2 GRAMMAR Advice, obligation, and expectation

	(Not) have to / Had better (not) / Be (not) supposed to	Base form of the verb		
Everyone	**has to**	come	to the meeting.	(It's required.)
You	**don't have to**	accept	that offer.	(You can walk away.)
I	**had better**	leave	now.	(I'm going to be late.)
You	**had better not**	be	late.	(The boss will be angry.)
I	**am supposed to**	call	them.	(They're expecting my call.)
We	**aren't supposed to**	use	our phones.	(It's against the rules.)

Notes
- *Had better (not)* often carries a suggestion of bad consequences.
- Use *have to* to say that an action is necessary / required.
- Use *(not) have to* to say that an action is not necessary.
- Use *had better (not)* to give strong advice or to talk about things people should or shouldn't do.
- Use *be (not) supposed to* to express expectations.

>> FOR PRACTICE, GO TO PAGE 150

3 PRONUNCIATION

A ▶09-08 Read and listen to the pronunciation note.

B ▶09-09 Listen. Notice how the underlined words are pronounced. Then listen again and repeat.

She <u>has to</u> sign a contract.

I <u>have to</u> leave.

<u>I'd better</u> leave now.

<u>You'd better not</u> go.

C ▶09-10 Listen and complete the sentences.

1. a. They _____ agree to that deal.
   b. They _____ agree to that deal.

2. a. You _____ reduce your price.
   b. You _____ reduce your price.

4 CONVERSATION

A ▶09-11 Listen or watch. What does Leti want Lan's advice about?

B ▶09-12 Listen or watch again. Answer the questions.

1. What job does the company want Leti to do?
2. Why is she not happy with the company?
3. What is Lan's advice?

C ▶09-13 FOCUS ON LANGUAGE Listen. Complete the conversation.

> **Leti:** They said I should put together a proposal—you know, with various options—and get back to them.
>
> **Lan:** That's a lot of work. And you may not even get the job. You _____ all that.
>
> **Leti:** Hmm. Maybe _____ .

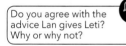

Do you agree with the advice Lan gives Leti? Why or why not?

5 TRY IT YOURSELF

A THINK Choose a situation. What could you offer in this negotiation? Make notes.

1. You work at a car dealership. Your boss told you not to accept less than $8,000 for a car, but the buyer wants a lower price. Negotiate with the buyer.
2. Your uncle gave you an ugly picture. You feel like you need to put it on the wall so he won't be offended when he comes over. You need to convince your roommate.

B ROLE PLAY With a partner, role-play the situations you chose. Explain what you have to, are supposed to, or had better do. Continue until you make a deal or walk away.

A: How much is this car?
B: It's $8,000.
A: I'll give you $7,000.
B: I'm sorry, I'm not supposed to reduce the price, but I can offer you a GPS system.

C ANALYZE Share the results of your negotiation with the class.

■ I CAN NEGOTIATE A DEAL.

LESSON 3 / DISCUSS NEGOTIATION SKILLS

LAN PHAM
@LanP

Just watched a talk about negotiation. I liked the part about listening to the other side—I need to remember that!

1 BEFORE YOU LISTEN

A ▶09-14 VOCABULARY Listen. Then listen and repeat.

> **naturally:** happening on its own, without people doing anything to make it happen
> **strength:** power
> **confidence:** the feeling that you are able to do things well
> **propose:** to suggest something
> **complicated:** having a lot of parts or being difficult to understand
> **an effort:** a determined try
> **realize:** to know or understand something you didn't know before

B Write answers to the questions.

1. What is something you are naturally good at? _____
2. What is your greatest strength? _____
3. How do people show confidence? _____
4. When was the last time you proposed an idea to a group? What was the idea?
   _____
5. What is something that takes a lot of effort? Why? _____
6. Name something complicated. Why is it complicated? _____
7. What is something you realized lately? _____

C PAIRS Ask and answer the questions in 1B.
   A: What is something you are naturally good at?
   B: I'm naturally good at fixing things. I've always liked to do that.
   A: Nice! I guess I'm naturally good at talking to people. I've never been shy.

2 GRAMMAR *Unless*

Use *unless* to express condition. *Unless* often means *if ... not*.

Unless	Subject	Present verb		Subject	Future verb or modal + verb	
	you	leave	soon,	you	are going to be	late.
Unless	the clients	trust	you,	they	won't want	your services.
	you	make	an effort,	you	can't	succeed.

Notes
- When the verb in the main clause is in the future, use the simple present in the clause with *if*.
- You can start the sentence with the main clause.
  We will meet at 9:00 unless the office is closed.

>> FOR PRACTICE, GO TO PAGE 151

3 LISTENING

A ▶09-15 Listen or watch. What is the speaker's main idea?

   a. A negotiation is more like a dance than a fight.
   b. You can win a negotiation if you are confident.
   c. Some people are naturally good at negotiating.

David Cruz I TSW Global Speaker Program
Unit 9: The negotiation dance

B ▶09-16 Read the Listening Skill. Listen or watch again. Complete the sentences with comparison words.

   1. _____ a dancer prepares for a performance by studying a set of steps, you need to prepare for a negotiation through research and planning.
   2. Good dancers pay close attention to their partners' moves. _____ , good negotiators listen to what their partners want.
   3. It takes confidence to smoothly move with your dance partner across the floor, and you'll need that _____ confidence when you negotiate.

> **LISTENING SKILL** Listen for comparisons
>
> When speakers are comparing two things, they may use words like these:
> | | |
> |---|---|
> | *same* | *(be) like* |
> | *similarly* | *just as* |
>
> Listen for these words to understand when something is being compared to something else.

C ▶09-17 Listen or watch again. Complete the sentences with the words in the box.

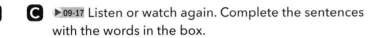

research	make sure	win	believe	improve	listen to

   1. You won't succeed if you think of a negotiation as a fight you want to _____ .
   2. You can _____ your skill at negotiating even if you aren't naturally good at it.
   3. You should _____ all of the facts before you begin a negotiation.
   4. It's very important to _____ what your partner wants.
   5. At the end of a negotiation, you want to _____ that both people are happy.
   6. If you have a lot of confidence, people will _____ in you.

D VOCABULARY EXPANSION Read the sentences from the talk. What do the underlined expressions mean?

   1. If you go into a negotiation focused on what *you* want and how *you* are going to get a better deal, <u>chances are</u> you won't be successful.
   2. Good negotiators listen to what their partners want. Unless you're working for that <u>win-win solution</u>, you'll never be a great negotiator.
   3. Groups almost always accept the solution proposed by the most confident person. Build your self-confidence; it's a very, very powerful tool in getting people to <u>see things your way</u>.

E PAIRS Compare your answers in 3D.

4 DISCUSSION

A THINK Imagine you're preparing for an important negotiation. How can you build your self-confidence? Make notes.

B DISCUSS In small groups, share your ideas in 4A.

C ANALYZE Discuss the ideas as a class. Talk about what the result might be if you don't do each thing.

You should *get a good night's sleep*. You won't think clearly unless you get enough sleep.

■ I CAN DISCUSS NEGOTIATION SKILLS.

LAN PHAM

@LanP

I took a quiz on my negotiation style. The results were pretty much what I expected. ☺

1 BEFORE YOU READ

A PAIRS How would you describe your personality? How does this affect your communication with others?

I'm very friendly, so I usually …

B ▶09-18 VOCABULARY Listen. Then listen and repeat. Do you know these words?

broad   a party   a middle ground   a position   on track   establish   partially

>> FOR DEFINITIONS AND PRACTICE, GO TO PAGE 151

2 READ

A PREVIEW Look at the title and the pictures. What do you think the magazine quiz says about negotiation styles?

B ▶09-19 Read and listen to the quiz. Were your predictions correct?

HOW DO YOU NEGOTIATE?

How do you negotiate? Are you too aggressive? Not aggressive enough? Experts have identified three broad styles of negotiation, and knowing what they are can help you become more aware of how you and others are communicating.

1 When you begin a negotiation, do you ___ ?

a get straight to business, without spending a lot of time trying to connect personally

b spend some time trying to connect with the other person

c focus on understanding what the other person wants before you talk about what you want

2 When the other party doesn't agree with you, do you ___ ?

a keep trying different ways to get what you want

b ask questions to make sure you really understand what the other person wants

c focus on trying to find a middle ground between your position and the other person's

3 When the negotiation is finished, are you mostly concerned about ___ ?

a whether you got what you wanted

b whether you and the other person have a good relationship

c whether you and the other person are both satisfied with the result

Two "a" answers: Competitive

A competitive negotiator is more focused on making the deal than building a relationship. You may be very successful at communicating what you want and at keeping the negotiation on track. On the negative side, competitive negotiators may be too aggressive. The other party may feel that their needs are not being recognized.

Two "b" answers: Cooperative

A cooperative negotiator is focused on having a good relationship with the other party. You are good at building trust with the other person and establishing a long-term relationship. However, you may focus too much on the other party's wishes and let them control the negotiation.

>>

> **Two "c" answers: Compromising**
A compromiser tries to arrive at a solution that leaves both parties partially satisfied with the results. A compromising style may allow you to conclude the negotiation without damaging the relationship. On the other hand, it may end up that neither side is completely happy with either the result of the negotiation or the relationship between the parties.

So, which kind of negotiator are you? Remember that different parts of a negotiation may require different styles. As with most areas of human communication, being aware of yourself and others is the key to success.

3 CHECK YOUR UNDERSTANDING

A Read the quiz again. What does the writer suggest about negotiating styles?
   a. Compromising negotiators get the best results because they listen to the other party.
   b. Different negotiating styles can be successful in different ways.
   c. When you negotiate, you should try to be both cooperative and compromising.

B Complete the sentences according to the quiz.
   1. If you start a negotiation by explaining exactly what you want, you probably have a _____ negotiating style.
   2. If you focus on finding things that you and the other party agree on, you probably have a _____ negotiating style.
   3. If you are concerned with making sure that the other person likes you, you probably have a _____ negotiating style.

C CLOSE READING Reread the description of a compromising negotiating style. Then circle the correct answers.
   1. What is being contrasted with *on the other hand*?
      a. a compromising negotiating style and a cooperative negotiating style
      b. the result of the negotiation and the relationship between the parties
      c. the good things about a compromising style and the negative results of this style
   2. What does the last sentence in the paragraph mean?
      a. One side is not happy with the results of the negotiation.
      b. Both sides are a little unhappy at the end of the negotiation.
      c. Both sides are happy with the relationship between the parties.

D Read the Reading Skill. Go back to the quiz. Make an inference about what the result of a negotiation might be if one person has a very competitive style.

> **READING SKILL Make inferences**
>
> As you read, use your own experience and previous knowledge to draw conclusions about things that the writer suggests but doesn't directly state. This is called making inferences.

E PAIRS What is the quiz about? Summarize the most important ideas. Use your own words.
   The quiz is about different negotiating styles ...

Take an online quiz. 🔍

4 MAKE IT PERSONAL

A Now take the quiz in 2B. Which style do you use the most? Which should you use more?
   My negotiating style: _____
   Style I should use more: _____
   Reason: _____

B PAIRS Compare your results and ideas in 4A.
   I am usually a competitive negotiator, but ...

☐ I CAN READ ABOUT NEGOTIATING STYLES.

LAN PHAM
@LanP

I like negotiating at work. I'm glad I don't have to do it at home!

1 BEFORE YOU WRITE

A Do you have any conflicts with the people you live or work with? How do you usually solve conflicts?

B Read the online advice column. What are Mei and Jen arguing about?

Problems at work or at home?
Just ask Ana!

Today's problem came in an email I received from Mei and Jen. I think it's a very common one for many people.

Mei and Jen are roommates and generally enjoy living with each other, but they have different ideas about cleaning and cooking. Mei likes to schedule weekly big cleanings because she doesn't like to clean every day. Jen prefers to tidy up as she goes. Also, Mei usually does the cooking and washes the dishes at night and thinks Jen should help more. Jen usually does the grocery shopping, so she thinks it's fair for Mei to cook and do the dishes. Mei and Jen are good friends and don't want to stop being roommates, but they are both losing their patience with each other.

So, what should they do? Luckily, there are a lot of ways to come to an agreement and go back to being happy roommates! First, Mei and Jen should get a monthly calendar and put it in a visible place in the apartment. Then Mei should say which two or three "big cleaning" tasks are the most important to her. Vacuuming? Cleaning the bathroom? Mei and Jen can decide together on which day those tasks get done and put it on the calendar. Then the other smaller tasks can be done when needed, which is Jen's style. As for the dinner conflict, Mei and Jen should try to do the grocery shopping together and then take turns cooking and cleaning. In that way, everyone pays their share for the groceries, and nobody spends too much time in the kitchen.

That's all for today. Come back tomorrow for another problem and solution.

C Read the advice column again. Complete the chart with information about the conflicts and the suggested solutions.

Conflicts

1.

2.

Mei's view

1.

2.

Jen's view

1.

2.

Solutions

1.

2.

2 FOCUS ON WRITING

Read the Writing Skill. Then go back to the advice column in 1B and underline Mei's point of view. Circle Jen's point of view.

3 PLAN YOUR WRITING

A Think of a conflict that you or someone you know has had with someone they live or work with. Complete the chart with information about the conflict, the points of view, and a possible solution.

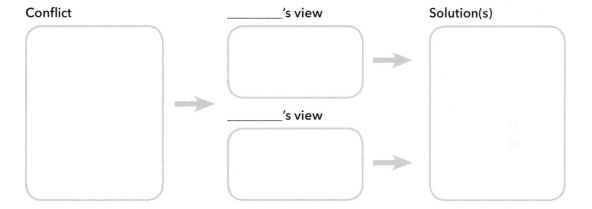

Conflict   _____'s view   Solution(s)

_____'s view

B PAIRS Talk about your ideas. Suggest ways your partner can improve or add to his or her ideas.

I understand the conflict but not one of the points of view ...

4 WRITE

Write about a conflict between people who live or work together, their points of view, and a suggested solution. Use the advice column in 1B as a model.

5 REVISE YOUR WRITING

A PAIRS Exchange and read each other's advice columns.

1. Underline the conflict. Is it clear what it is?
2. Label each person's point of view with A and B. Can you understand why the person thinks and feels the way he or she does?
3. Does the suggested solution help each person to feel better?

Revising tip

When revising your draft, focus on content and organization, not mechanics.

B PAIRS Can your partner improve his or her advice column? Make suggestions.

6 PROOFREAD

Read your advice column again. Check your

- spelling
- punctuation
- capitalization

■ I CAN WRITE ABOUT A CONFLICT.

PUT IT TOGETHER

1 PRESENTATION PROJECT

A ▶09-20 Listen or watch. What is the topic of the presentation?

_____

B ▶09-21 Listen or watch again. Answer the questions.

1. Why does Misaki say self-confidence is important?

_____

2. What are Misaki's three suggestions for developing confidence?

_____

C Read the Presentation Skill. What are some ways that you can practice speaking loudly and clearly?

D Make your own presentation.

Step 1 In Lesson 3, you heard a speaker compare negotiating to a dance and say that you need confidence to negotiate. Search for advice about developing confidence for negotiations. Which suggestions do you think are most useful? Make a list.

> ### PRESENTATION SKILL
>
> **Use a loud, clear voice**
> Speak loudly and pronounce words clearly so all your audience members can hear and understand you.

Step 2 Prepare a two-minute presentation about suggestions for developing confidence for a negotiation.

Step 3 Give your presentation to the class. Remember to speak loudly and clearly. Answer questions and get feedback.

> How did you do? Complete the self-evaluation on page 165.

2 REFLECT AND PLAN

A Look back through the unit. Check (✓) the things you learned. Highlight the things you need to learn.

Speaking objectives
- ☐ Talk about a past negotiation
- ☐ Negotiate a deal
- ☐ Discuss negotiation skills

Vocabulary
- ☐ People at a conference
- ☐ Verbs for negotiating

Conversation
- ☐ End a phone call

Pronunciation
- ☐ _Have to, has to, had better (not)_

Listening
- ☐ Listen for comparisons

Grammar
- ☐ Causative verbs: _get, have,_ and _make_
- ☐ Advice, obligation, and expectation
- ☐ _Unless_

Reading
- ☐ Make inferences

Writing
- ☐ Explain different points of view

B What will you do to learn the things you highlighted? For example, use your app, review your Student Book, or do other practice. Make a plan.

> Notes   Done
>
> Review the grammar in Lesson 1, page 102.
> _____
> _____
> _____

10 HOW'S SHE DOING?

GET STARTED

A Read the unit title and the learning goals.

B Look at the photo. What's going on?

C Now read Ed's message. What does Ed want advice about?

ED MILLER
@EdM

Excited about my new job on the social media team! Got any advice about getting along with new co-workers?

LESSON 1   TALK ABOUT A CONVERSATION

ED MILLER
@EdM

New York is a big city but a small world. You'll never guess who I ran into today!

1 VOCABULARY Explaining and arguing

A ▶10-01 Listen. Then listen and repeat.

I didn't see the red light!
an excuse

Why don't you try this one?
a suggestion

I just thought of something!
an idea

The e is silent.
like
an explanation

I disagree!
a disagreement

It's too cold!
a complaint

This isn't on sale today.
Good point. Let's not buy it now.
a point

B ▶10-02 Listen to the conversations. Complete the sentences with the words in 1A.

1. The student has a good _____ .
2. The customer has _____ .
3. The salesperson has _____ .
4. The woman thinks the man has _____ .
5. The woman has _____ .
6. The teacher is giving _____ .
7. They are having _____ .

C PAIRS Choose three of the things in 1A and tell your partner an example from your life.

I had an excuse when I was late for work last week. My car broke down.

2 GRAMMAR Embedded yes / no questions

Report a *yes / no* question by embedding it in a sentence with a form of the verb *ask + if* or *whether*.

Direct yes / no question		Embedded question		
		If / whether	Subject	Verb
Are you enjoying your job?	She asked (me)	**whether**	**I**	**was enjoying** my job.
Do you have any suggestions?	He asked (us)	**if**	**we**	**had** any suggestions.
Can you give me an explanation?	She asked (them)	**whether**	**they**	**could give** her an explanation.
Note Use statement word order in the embedded question.				

>> FOR PRACTICE, GO TO PAGE 152

3 CONVERSATION SKILL

A ▶10-03 Read the conversation skill. Listen. Notice how the speaker accepts the apology.

1. A: I'm so sorry about that!
   B: That's OK. No harm done.
2. A: Please accept my apology.
   B: It's all right. I understand.

<table>
<tr><td colspan="2">Accept an apology</td></tr>
<tr><td colspan="2">Use phrases like these to accept an apology:</td></tr>
<tr><td>That's OK.</td><td>No harm done.</td></tr>
<tr><td>It's all right.</td><td>Don't worry about it.</td></tr>
<tr><td>No problem.</td><td>I understand.</td></tr>
</table>

B PAIRS Use the sentences to apologize. Take turns accepting the apologies. Use the language from the conversation skill box.

1. I'm so sorry I'm late!
2. Please accept my apology. I had an emergency at home, and I forgot our appointment.
3. I feel terrible I forgot your birthday! I'm so sorry!

4 CONVERSATION

A ▶10-04 Listen or watch. What are they talking about?

a. Ed's problems at work
b. Ed's conversation with Pam
c. Ed's new job

B ▶10-05 Listen or watch again. Answer the questions.

1. How does Pam feel about law school?
2. What plan did Ed and Pam make?
3. Why doesn't Ed know Pam well?

C ▶10-06 FOCUS ON LANGUAGE Listen. Complete the conversation.

> Ed: Oh, and she asked _____ with the new website. I told her we'd only gotten a few complaints.
>
> Ahmet: Just a few!
>
> Ed: Yeah. I told her that we're working on it. And I asked _____ for working with Charles.

What do Ahmet and Ed think about Pam? What do they think about Charles? What makes someone a good co-worker or classmate?

5 TRY IT YOURSELF

A THINK Think about a time when you saw or talked to someone you hadn't seen in a long time. What did you talk about? What questions did you ask? What questions did the person ask you? Make a list.

B PAIRS Tell a partner about your conversation.

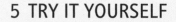

I saw an old friend of mine in a café the other day. I asked if she still lived near here. She asked me whether I had quit my job.

C ANALYZE Tell the class about your conversation. Did any of the conversations include a complaint, a suggestion, or an explanation?

■ I CAN TALK ABOUT A CONVERSATION.

ED MILLER
@EdM

It's so frustrating when people make excuses!

1 VOCABULARY Interacting with others

A Look at the chart. Do you ever have problems like these with co-workers or classmates? What else would you add to this list?

SURVEY RESULTS: The Most Annoying Co-Worker Behaviors	1. blames others for mistakes	2. comes in late and leaves early	3. never admits to being wrong	4. makes drama out of everything	5. constantly tries to get the boss's approval	6. criticizes others behind their backs

B ▶10-07 Listen. Then listen and repeat.

> **meet up:** to come to the same place as someone because you have planned this
> **run into:** to meet someone when you were not expecting to
> **get along (with):** to have a friendly relationship with someone
> **agree with:** to have the same opinion as someone else
> **disagree with:** to have a different opinion from someone else
> **speak up:** to say publicly what you think about something
> **join in:** to begin to take part in an activity that other people are involved in
> **take care of:** to give people the things they need

C Write answers to the questions.

1. Who was the last person you met up with? _____
2. What kind of people do you get along with? _____
3. Do you usually speak up when you're upset about something? _____
4. What was the most surprising place you ran into someone? _____
5. Who have you had to take care of? _____
6. If your friends were running a race, would you want to join in? _____

D PAIRS Ask and answer the questions in 1C.

2 GRAMMAR Questions with final prepositions

For questions with phrasal verbs, the preposition usually goes at the end of the question.

Statement			Question			
Subject	Verb + preposition	Object	Question word (object)	Auxiliary verb	Subject	Verb + preposition
We	talked about	the website.	What	did	you	talk about?
They	are looking at	the picture.	What	are	they	looking at?
He	takes care of	the clients.	Who	does	he	take care of?

>> **FOR PRACTICE, GO TO PAGE 153**

3 PRONUNCIATION

A ▶10-08 Read and listen to the pronunciation note.

B ▶10-09 Listen. Notice how the verbs and prepositions are linked. Then listen again and repeat.

What did you talk‿about?

Don't come‿in late.

Paula takes care‿of the clients.

C ▶10-10 Listen and complete the sentences. Then practice the conversations with a partner.

1. A: Did you _____ with Marco?
   B: Yeah. I _____ him this morning.
2. A: What was your boss _____ ?
   B: I _____ late–again.
3. A: _____ , let's go!
   B: I'm coming! I'm coming!

4 CONVERSATION

A ▶10-11 Listen or watch. Why is Ed upset?

B ▶10-12 Listen or watch again. Answer the questions.

1. What did the tech team say about the problem?
2. What does Paula think Ed should do?
3. What does Ed decide to do in the end?

C ▶10-13 FOCUS ON LANGUAGE Listen. Complete the conversation.

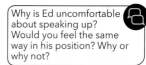

Why is Ed uncomfortable about speaking up? Would you feel the same way in his position? Why or why not?

Paula:	Oh, yeah! I ran into Marta from customer service in the lobby this morning and she told me a customer had had problems finding some information on the website.
Ed:	What was _____ ?
Paula:	The contact information for the Beijing office.

5 TRY IT YOURSELF

A THINK about a time when you felt you had to speak up about something important to you or something you didn't agree with. Make notes.

B PAIRS Ask and answer questions about your memories.

A: When did you speak up?
B: My manager hadn't given me a raise. I spoke up and he raised my salary!

C COMPARE Share with the class. Who had the most difficult time speaking up?

▇ I CAN DISCUSS A DIFFICULT INTERACTION.

DISCUSS DEALING WITH DIFFICULT PEOPLE

ED MILLER
@EdM

I saw a talk about dealing with difficult people. It had some good advice. Maybe I should take a walk in the park.

1 BEFORE YOU LISTEN

  A ▶10-14 VOCABULARY Listen. Then listen and repeat.

He wants to **escape**.

They are **reacting** with surprise.

She is **respectful** to her grandmother.

The nurse has **sympathy** for the patient.

The bear is **comforting** to the child.

She is **demanding** her food right now.

The child is being **unreasonable**.

He is too **emotional**. He needs to calm down.

B Read the definitions. Write the words from 1A.

1. _____ : a sad feeling for someone when something bad is happening to him or her
2. _____ : behaving in a polite way
3. _____ : showing strong feelings
4. _____ : to get away from a place or person
5. _____ : making someone feel less worried or unhappy
6. _____ : acting in a particular way because something has happened
7. _____ : not willing to listen to facts or follow good advice
8. _____ : asking for something in a strong way

C PAIRS Use the words in 1A to write sentences about your own life. Then share your sentences.

A: My cat escaped from the house the other day.
B: Sometimes I want to escape from work!

2 GRAMMAR Repeated and parallel comparatives

Use a repeated comparative to show something increasing or getting bigger or stronger.

They are making your life	**more and more stressful.**
The work is getting	**easier and easier.**

Use a parallel comparative to show a result.

The	Comparative adjective		*The*	Comparative adjective	
The	faster	you drive,	the	more dangerous	it is.
The	more emotional	he gets,	the	more unreasonable	he will be.

>> FOR PRACTICE, GO TO PAGE 154

3 LISTENING

A ▶10-15 Listen or watch. What is the purpose of the talk?

a. to help you teach difficult people how to change their behavior

b. to give you ideas for controlling your reactions to difficult people

c. to explain why difficult people behave the way they do

Adriana Lopez | TSW Global Speaker Program
Unit 10: When people are the problem

B ▶10-16 Read the Listening Skill. Listen or watch again. Complete the sentences with words that signal importance.

1. It's not the easiest advice to follow, but it might help lower your stress. _____, stay calm.

2. It is _____ important not to argue with unreasonable people.

> **LISTENING SKILL**
> **Listen for words that signal importance**
>
> Speakers often use expressions like these to show that something is important:
> *most importantly   particularly*
> *especially*
> Listen for these expressions to understand what the speaker thinks is important.

C ▶10-17 Listen or watch again. Complete the sentences with the words in the box.

respectful   stress   demand
listen to   take care of   understand

1. Difficult people are a major source of _____ in the workplace.

2. It's important to really _____ difficult people, and be _____.

3. Don't say that you _____ .

4. Don't _____ that the person change his or her behavior.

5. After you have dealt with a difficult person, you need to _____ your own stress.

D VOCABULARY EXPANSION Read the sentences from the talk. What do the underlined expressions mean?

1. If you haven't done anything wrong, don't be afraid to <u>stand up for yourself</u> and say, "Please don't talk to me like that."

2. Smiling too much can <u>backfire</u>. The person may feel that you're laughing at them.

3. If you got through an encounter with a difficult person and didn't <u>lose your cool</u>, you also need to congratulate yourself. Keeping calm isn't always easy.

E PAIRS Compare your answers in 3D.

4 DISCUSSION

A THINK about a time you dealt with a difficult person. What was the problem? What did they do? What did you do? Make notes.

B DISCUSS Share your experiences in a small group. What did people do that made the situations better? What made them worse? Would anyone do anything differently?

I tried to argue with him, and he just got more and more upset.
I listened to her story, and the calmer I was, the calmer she got, too.

C ANALYZE Share with the class. Would the advice in the talk have helped in the situations you discussed in your groups? Why or why not?

■ I CAN DISCUSS DEALING WITH DIFFICULT PEOPLE.

ED MILLER
@EdM

This book is so inspiring. I think I might start doing volunteer work!

1 BEFORE YOU READ

A   PAIRS   When was the last time you helped somebody? What did you do?

Last weekend I helped my brother ...

B   ▶10-18 VOCABULARY   Listen. Then listen and repeat. Do you know these words?

> altruism   a donation   a sacrifice   constant   humanity
> **>> FOR DEFINITIONS AND PRACTICE, GO TO PAGE 154**

2 READ

A   PREVIEW   Look at the title and the pictures. What do you think the book is about?

B   ▶10-19   Read and listen to the book review. Were your predictions correct?

Book Review:

Strangers Drowning

★★★★★

Reviewer: Ken Barton

A man gives so much of his salary to the poor that he has to look through garbage bins to feed himself. A middle-class couple with two children adopts 20 more, many of them with special needs. A woman donates her kidney to a total stranger. These people are extreme altruists. They don't
5   just make a small monthly donation or volunteer every other week. They make serious, often life-long, sacrifices to help others, and they are the subject of Larissa MacFarquhar's book *Strangers Drowning*.

The title of this book may make you think of a hero who jumps into a river to rescue a drowning stranger, but extreme altruism is not the same as a
10   one-time action. Most of us can understand why people do something heroic in an emergency. It's much harder to understand people who choose to make constant sacrifices. They make us feel uncomfortable; we suspect there is something not quite right with them. MacFarquhar's book explores extreme altruism in detail.

15   So, why do many people feel so uncomfortable about extreme altruism? Shouldn't we be glad about someone helping others? Part of the reason we have these attitudes is that we like our comforts and don't want to feel bad about enjoying them. We also may feel overwhelmed by the huge number of people in the world who need help. But MacFarquhar
20   explains another reason: Most of us really aren't sure if these people are doing the right thing. We believe that it's important to put family or community before strangers, and extreme altruists don't do that. For example, the woman who donated her kidney put her own health at risk, which could affect those who love her.

25   MacFarquhar shows that extreme altruists don't understand why the person drowning in front of us is considered more important than the one drowning on the other side of the world. They believe that the best way to live life is to help as many people as possible.

What makes this book so interesting is that it's not just a group of stories
30   about extreme altruists. MacFarquhar spends much of it discussing the deeper issues around how these people live and think and what that means for the rest of us. It is a fascinating, complex, and intelligent look at humanity—definitely worth your time.

3 CHECK YOUR UNDERSTANDING

A Read the review again. Why does the writer think people should read this book?

a. It discusses important ideas about humanity.

b. It explains what is wrong with extreme altruists.

c. It tells interesting stories about heroic acts.

B Circle the correct answers, according to the article.

1. By *extreme altruist*, the writer means a person who ___ .

   a. jumps into a river to save a drowning stranger

   b. makes long-term difficult sacrifices for others

   c. volunteers at food banks and makes monthly donations

2. Some people believe that extreme altruists ___ .

   a. may actually be hurting people instead of helping them

   b. are not sacrificing as much as they say they are

   c. are helping strangers instead of friends and family

3. Extreme altruists believe that ___ .

   a. it's more important to help a lot of people than to just help the people you know

   b. we should help our own communities before we help others

   c. it's never worth it to put families and friends at risk

C CLOSE READING Reread lines 29–33. Then circle the correct answers.

1. What does the first sentence mean?

   a. The book does not have many stories about extreme altruists, but it is still interesting.

   b. The stories about extreme altruists in the book are not very interesting.

   c. The book is interesting because it includes more than stories about extreme altruists.

2. What does *what that means for the rest of us* mean?

   a. what extreme altruists can learn from MacFarquhar's discussion

   b. what other people can learn from the behavior of extreme altruists

   c. what the stories tell the reader about extreme altruists

D Read the Reading Skill. Go back to the book review in 2B. Underline two examples of words that introduce Larissa MacFarquhar's ideas (not Ken Barton's ideas).

E PAIRS What is the book review about? Summarize the most important ideas. Use your own words.

The review discusses a book about extreme altruists ...

> **READING SKILL Identify paraphrasing**
>
> Writers often explain other people's ideas without quoting them directly. They put the ideas in their own words and use verbs like *explain, show, discuss, question,* and *argue* to introduce them. These words help the reader understand which ideas come from another source.

Find an example of extreme altruism. 🔍

4 MAKE IT PERSONAL

A Think of someone you know (or know of) who helps a lot of people. Take notes in the chart.

Name / occupation	
How the person has helped people	
Sacrifices the person has made	

B PAIRS Compare your ideas in 4A. Do you want to be more like this person? Why or why not?

I would like to be more like my friend because he ...

☐ I CAN READ ABOUT EXTREME ALTRUISM.

LESSON 5 WRITE ABOUT A KINDNESS

ED MILLER
@EdM

With so much bad news in the world, it's nice to read something about people being kind to each other!

1 BEFORE YOU WRITE

A Have you ever experienced an act of kindness from a stranger? Have you ever performed an act of kindness for a stranger?

B Read the personal essay about an act of kindness. Why was Andrew feeling sad?

A Stranger's Kindness

by Andrew Reynolds

Last year, I learned that a small kindness from a stranger can really make a difference in a person's life. This is what happened.

I was sitting in a small café, drinking coffee. Having just broken up with my girlfriend of two years, I was feeling pretty down. To make things worse, I had recently quit my job and moved to her town so we could live closer to each other. So I had no girlfriend and no job. To top it all off, it was my 30th birthday and I had no one to celebrate with.

So there I was, alone in a busy café watching groups of friends, happy couples, and laughing families enjoying their time together. At that moment, I felt like I had never been sadder. A server, having noticed me sitting alone, came over and asked me if everything was OK. I had no one else to talk to, so I told her my depressing story. She said she was sorry and went back to work.

After another 20 minutes or so, I went to the counter to pay. Instead of taking my money, she told me my lunch was free and started singing "Happy Birthday." Then everyone in the café joined in! All of a sudden, I wasn't so lonely.

I went back to the café the next day, and now I am a regular customer. Some of the other people from that day are regulars, too, and they're now my friends. It's amazing how a small act of kindness can make such a big difference in someone's life!

C Read the personal essay again. Complete the chart with information about what happened.

Who?	Where?	When?

What was the situation?	What happened next?	How did it end?

2 FOCUS ON WRITING

Read the Writing Skill. Look at the sentences from the personal essay. Then reread the text and write numbers 1–6 to show the order in which things happened.

____ He went to the counter to pay.

____ The server noticed him sitting alone.

____ The server came over and asked if everything was OK.

____ He broke up with his girlfriend.

____ He was sitting in a small café, drinking coffee.

____ He quit his job and moved to a new town.

> **WRITING SKILL**
> **Use past tenses to show sequence**
>
> When writing a personal essay, it is important to make sure the sequence of events is clear to the reader. Writers often use simple past, past continuous, and *having* + past participle to tell the order of events in the story.

3 PLAN YOUR WRITING

A Think of a time when someone was kind to you or you were kind to someone. Complete the chart with the information and events in the order they happened.

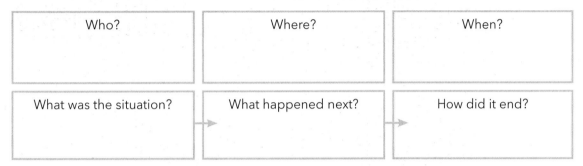

Who?	Where?	When?

What was the situation?	What happened next?	How did it end?

B PAIRS Talk about your ideas. Suggest ways your partner can improve or add to his or her ideas.

I like your story, but I'm not sure when this event happened …

4 WRITE

Write about a time when someone was kind to you or you were kind to someone. Make sure you use the correct tenses so the sequence of events is clear. Use the personal essay in 1B as a model.

> **Drafting tip**
> When you write your first draft, you don't have to start at the beginning of the story. You can start anywhere.

5 REVISE YOUR WRITING

A PAIRS Exchange and read each other's essays.

1. Underline the person who performed the act of kindness.
2. Number the events in the order they happened. Is the sequence clear? Is the use of tenses correct?
3. Do you understand why the act of kindness made the person feel better?

B PAIRS Can your partner improve his or her personal essay? Make suggestions.

6 PROOFREAD

Read your personal essay again. Check your

- spelling
- punctuation
- capitalization

■ I CAN WRITE ABOUT A KINDNESS.

PUT IT TOGETHER

1 PRESENTATION PROJECT

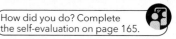

A ▶10-20 Listen or watch. What is the topic of the presentation?

B ▶10-21 Listen or watch again. Answer the questions.

1. Who is Junio talking about? _____

2. How are the two friends different from each other? _____

3. What uncomfortable interactions does Junio talk about? _____

4. What does Junio say he appreciates? _____

C Read the Presentation Skill. Make a list of ways that you can end a presentation positively.

D Make your own presentation.

Step 1 Think about someone you appreciate even though the person's personality is different from yours.

- Who is it? How did you meet?
- How are they different from you?
- Have these differences caused any difficult interactions?
- What do you appreciate about this person?

Step 2 Prepare a two-minute presentation about your relationship with this person.

Step 3 Give your presentation to the class. Remember to end your presentation positively. Answer questions and get feedback.

> **PRESENTATION SKILL**
>
> **End your presentation positively**
> At the end of your presentation, say your last sentence with confidence, then smile and wait for your audience to clap. Remain standing and invite the audience to ask questions if you have time.

How did you do? Complete the self-evaluation on page 165.

2 REFLECT AND PLAN

A Look back through the unit. Check (✓) the things you learned. Highlight the things you need to learn.

Speaking objectives
- ☐ Talk about a conversation
- ☐ Discuss a difficult interaction
- ☐ Discuss dealing with difficult people

Vocabulary
- ☐ Explaining and arguing
- ☐ Interacting with others

Conversation
- ☐ Accept an apology

Pronunciation
- ☐ Linking verbs to prepositions

Listening
- ☐ Listen for words that signal importance

Grammar
- ☐ Embedded *yes / no* questions
- ☐ Questions with final prepositions
- ☐ Repeated and parallel comparatives

Reading
- ☐ Identify paraphrasing

Writing
- ☐ Use past tenses to show sequence

B What will you do to learn the things you highlighted? For example, use your app, review your Student Book, or do other practice. Make a plan.

‹ Notes   Done

Review the vocabulary in Lesson 1, page 114.
_____
_____
_____
_____

A Complete the text message conversation about a day at the beach. Use the phrases in the box.

get done   ~~getting hot~~   got soaked   get damaged   getting excited   get nervous

Hi Oscar! It was __getting hot__
1
in my apartment, so here I am at the beach!

Lucky you! I have so much work to _____ ! So, have you been in
2
the water yet? Don't _____,
3
but I think there are sharks at that beach.

No, there aren't! The water was wonderful, but I forgot to take off my smart watch. It _____ !
4

Those are expensive! I hope it didn't
_____.
5

No, I think it's OK. I brought a mystery novel with me, and I'm _____ about reading it under the sun!
6

B Complete the email about a concert. Use the words in the box and the correct form of *get*.

confused   damaged   hurt   ~~better~~   cloudy   wet

New email

Hi Lela!

I went to see the group Dark Dream in concert yesterday. They weren't very good when I saw them a few years ago, but they __have gotten better__ since then. They started playing, and it was
1
awesome! Unfortunately, it started _____, and after a few songs, it started to rain.
2
The equipment and the stage _____, but they didn't stop playing. At one point,
3
while the singer was running around the stage, he _____ about where he was,
4
and he fell into the crowd! Fortunately, the audience caught him, so he _____.
5
It stopped raining for the second half of the concert. I wanted to send you some pictures, but my
smart phone _____ at the concert somehow 😞.
6
See you tomorrow,

Dario

C MAKE IT PERSONAL Imagine you ran in a race. Write about your experience. Use a form of *get* + the adjective or past participle in parentheses.

1. (**nervous**) I got nervous when I learned it might rain.
2. (**thirsty**) _____
3. (**scared**) _____
4. (**hurt**) _____
5. (**lost**) _____
6. (**excited**) _____

UNIT 1, LESSON 2 *SO* AND *SUCH*

A Complete the email about a vacation. Use *so* or *such*.

New email

Hi Tom!

We arrived in Florida yesterday, and we're already having _____such_____ a great time. The weather

is _____ nice here! I'm wearing shorts, a T-shirt, and sandals. It's _____ a nice
  2   3

change from all the snow back home in New York. Our hotel is right on the beach, and the view

is _____ beautiful that I never want to leave. Today we visited a wildlife park where the
  4

animals aren't kept in cages. It was _____ a strange feeling to drive by elephants and lions
                                      5

in Florida! The lions got _____ close to the windows that we could see their huge teeth!
                          6

We're planning to go to Disney World tomorrow. Everybody's _____ excited!
                                                             7

Take care!

Anna

B Complete the blog post about an elephant sanctuary in Thailand. Use *so* or *such*
and the words in parentheses. Add *a* or *an* if necessary.

I think saving the elephants of Thailand is ____such an important____
                                             1 (important)
project. Elephants are _____ and intelligent animals.
                        2 (beautiful)
I flew to Thailand from my home in England last month to visit a wildlife

park just for elephants. It was _____ flight, but I was
                                3 (long)
_____ to get there! There were 30 rescued elephants
   4 (excited)
living in the park. It's _____ area for elephants,
                         5 (perfect)
with fields, hills, and even a small river for them to enjoy. The staff were

_____ to the elephants; they even made a birthday
      6 (kind)
cake for one of them. I've never seen _____ cake! If
                                         7 (big)
you love elephants like I do, why not send a small donation to the center?

It's _____ way to help the elephants of Thailand.
     8 (great)

C MAKE IT PERSONAL Complete the comments with phrases beginning with *so* or *such*.

1. Elephants are amazing because they are _such sensitive and intelligent animals_____.
2. Seeing a lion in the wild would be _____.
3. Being a nature photographer must be _____.
4. Creating animal conservation areas is _____.
5. Learning about endangered species is _____.
6. Swimming with hippos is _____.
7. It is important to protect bees because they are _____.

UNIT 1, LESSON 3   *THOUGH, ALTHOUGH,* AND *EVEN THOUGH*

A Combine the sentences using the words in parentheses. Don't change the order of the clauses.

1. Many people talk about endangered animals.
    Few do anything about the problem. (although)
    Many people talk about endangered animals, although few do anything about the problem.

2. The wolf looked just like my dog. (though)
    It had no collar.
    _____

3. The oceans seem limitless. (even though)
    We must put limits on fishing.
    _____

4. Wild animals can be adorable.
    Most make terrible pets. (although)
    _____

5. It was wearing a GPS collar. (though)
    We don't know where the elephant is.
    _____

6. Controlled burning of forests can help protect trees.
    It may seem like it harms them. (even though)
    _____

B MAKE IT PERSONAL Complete the sentences by adding a clause with *although*, *though*, or *even though*. Remember to use commas correctly.

1. Cockroaches aren't endangered animals, *although many people wish they were* _____.
2. A surprising number of animals live in the city _____.
3. _____ I've never actually seen one.
4. Roads are a great danger for many animals _____.

UNIT 1, LESSON 4 VOCABULARY PRACTICE

Read the definitions. Then complete the sentences with the words.

> **orphaned:** not having any parents
> **fascinating:** very interesting
> **an enclosure:** an area that is surrounded by walls or a fence, and may also have a roof
> **an environment:** the place and the things around you that influence how you feel
> **mimic:** to copy the way someone or something looks, talks, walks, or moves
> **a natural habitat:** the place where a plant or animal lives in nature

1. I can _____ my brother's voice. My mother can't tell the difference!
2. The zoo tries to reproduce each animal's _____.
3. The lions' _____ must be very big so they have room to move around.
4. Julia had to feed the _____ kittens because they had no mother.
5. This book about Jane Goodall is _____! I can't stop reading it.
6. The office _____ terrible. Everyone is miserable.

UNIT 2, LESSON 1 REPORTED SPEECH

A Complete Sonia's blog post about being positive and welcoming new challenges. Use the words and phrases in the box.

> could   had   was hoping   wouldn't   ~~didn't match~~   had been

At my interview with my company, the manager mentioned that my skills and experience __*didn't match*__ the job description exactly. I didn't let
1
that bother me. I told him that I _____ mind learning on the job.
2
Then he said it was only a short-term position. I told him that, actually,

I _____ for a permanent position. He thought for a moment.
3
Then he said he _____ probably find one for me. After I got the
4
job, he told me that he _____ interviewed 100 candidates, and
5
he said it _____ my positive attitude that had made the difference.
6

B Read what Joya's new boss Sylvia said on Joya's first day. Then rewrite Sylvia's statements as reported speech, using the verbs in parentheses.

1. "I didn't expect you to get here so early." (mention)
   <u>She mentioned that she hadn't expected me to get there so early.</u>

2. "I think you're doing a great job!" (tell)
   _____

3. "I've never seen anyone learn so fast!" (tell)
   _____

4. "The company made a great decision when they chose you." (say)
   _____

5. "I'll take you to lunch later if you're free." (say)
   _____

6. "You deserve a permanent position." (tell)
   _____

C MAKE IT PERSONAL Imagine something a co-worker told you about the workplace. First write the information using direct speech. Then write it in reported speech. Use the reporting verbs and the verb tense changes in parentheses.

1. (*say*, simple present → simple past)
   a. <u>He said, "There's a new coffee machine."</u>
   b. <u>He said (that) there was a new coffee machine.</u>

2. (*say*, past → past perfect)
   a. _____
   b. _____

3. (*tell*, present continuous → past continuous)
   a. _____
   b. _____

UNIT 2, LESSON 2   DEFINING RELATIVE CLAUSES

A Complete Jim's blog post about a first job. Use relative pronouns and the correct form of the words in parentheses to write defining relative clauses.

My first job was at the golf course _____**that was near**_____
1 (be / near)
my house. My father had seen a sign

_____ "Help Wanted" and suggested I
2 (say)
apply for the job. When I filled out the application, they said

they were looking for someone _____
3 (have)
good communication skills and was responsible. I told them

I was the guy _____! The part of the job
4 (they / look for)
_____ was cleaning because the golf
5 (I / not / like)
club was really big. But I really enjoyed giving tours to people

_____ to join the club. Some of the players _____ were
6 (want)   **7 (join)**
professional golfers. I still have a book of golfers' signatures _____ while
8 (I / collect)
I was working there.

B Read the statements. Then combine them into one sentence with a defining relative clause. More than one answer may be possible.

1. Some people have good leadership skills. Those people are usually good managers.
   People who have good leadership skills are usually good managers.

2. I just got out of a meeting. It was about new clients.
   _____

3. Employees have good technical skills. Those employees need to be paid well.
   _____

4. I'm looking for an assistant. That assistant can work independently.
   _____

5. The company hired my friend Louis. I work for the company.
   _____

6. The candidates have good communication skills. Those candidates will be successful.
   _____

C MAKE IT PERSONAL Complete the sentences with defining relative clauses and your ideas.

1. It's a bad idea to hire someone _who isn't positive or responsible_____.
2. People _____ are the kind of people I like to work with.
3. I'm the kind of worker _____.
4. I'd prefer to work for a company _____.
5. I'd like to have a position _____.
6. I'd be the kind of boss _____.
7. I think someone _____ could be a successful salesperson.

UNIT 2, LESSON 3 *SO* AND *THEREFORE*

A Combine the sentences using *so* or *therefore*. Don't change the order of the clauses. Use a comma or semicolon as needed.

1. You can make a deposit at the ATM. You don't need to see a bank teller. (so)
   <u>You can make a deposit at the ATM, so you don't need to see a bank teller.</u>

2. The company is expanding. They are hiring more engineers. (therefore)
   _____

3. Keith used to be a landscaper. He knows a lot about plants. (so)
   _____

4. Maya will graduate next month. She is interviewing for jobs now. (so)
   _____

5. The tax laws have changed this year. We should talk to an accountant. (therefore)
   _____

6. The printer is broken again. We have to call the technician. (so)
   _____

B MAKE IT PERSONAL Use *so* or *therefore* to make a conclusion. Add a comma before *so* or a period before *therefore*.

1. Cybersecurity is a growing industry <u>. Therefore, it is a good career choice.</u>
2. Automation will eliminate the need for some current jobs _____
3. A technician fixed the copy machine _____
4. Self-driving vehicles are becoming more popular _____

UNIT 2, LESSON 4 VOCABULARY PRACTICE

Read the definitions. Then complete the sentences with the words.

> **a passion:** a strong liking for something
> **a salary:** money that you get for the job you do
> **satisfaction:** a feeling of happiness because you got something you wanted
> **clergy:** religious leaders
> **a psychologist:** someone who has studied the mind and how it affects behavior
> **a connection:** a usually good relationship between people, things, ideas, etc.
> **a dead end:** a situation where no progress, or moving forward, is possible
> **take pride in:** to have a feeling of happiness or pleasure in what you have done
> **spare time:** free time; time when you are not working
> **donate:** to give money or things to help others

1. Her _____ is working with people, so she decided to become a _____.
2. If you don't do something useful every day, you won't have _____ in your work.
3. I have no _____ to volunteer but I try to _____ money to charity when I can.
4. I don't think I can get a promotion at my company. It's a _____.
5. The _____ will lead the memorial service.
6. My best friend and I became friends right away. We felt a strong _____.
7. My father always tells me to _____ even the smallest tasks.
8. His _____ is much higher at his new job. He just bought a new car.

UNIT 3, LESSON 1 SUPERLATIVE ADJECTIVES

A Complete the email about a trip. Use the superlative form of the adjectives in parentheses.

New email

Hi Sarah!

I'm still on vacation in Los Angeles. I think it's among ___the most interesting___ places in the world!
1 (interesting)

I've been all over the city—this must be one of _____ vacations I've ever taken.
2 (busy)

I love the food here! I've eaten at some of _____ restaurants in the city. I also
3 (good)

went to a cool food fair, and I had some of _____ cookies I've ever eaten. They
4 (big)

were so good! And you should see Venice Beach. I think it's among _____
5 (beautiful)

beaches in the world. One of _____ things was looking for movie stars on
6 (exciting)

the beach. I think I saw Leonardo DiCaprio! The only thing I don't like here is driving. They have

_____ traffic I've ever seen!
7 (crazy)

I have to go now. We'll talk when I get back!

Norah

B Complete the advertisement for a school festival. Use the words in parentheses to write superlative expressions.

C MAKE IT PERSONAL Complete the sentences. Use information and superlatives that are true for you.

1. I think ___Picasso___ is one of ___the greatest___ artists who ever lived.

2. I think _____ is one of _____ cities in the world.

3. In my opinion, _____ is one of _____ languages.

4. I think _____ is among _____ places on earth.

5. I'd say _____ is one of _____ restaurants in town.

6. One of _____ actors alive today is _____.

Join us for the Hillfield High School
International Festival THIS WEEKEND! ★

- The festival will be held in Dunton Park, ___one of the most beautiful___ parks in the country.
  1 (one / beautiful)
- We'll have _____ Japanese
  2 (some / delicious)
  food in the city, and for dessert, you'll enjoy
  _____ fruits from around
  3 (some / sweet)
  the world—with ice cream!
- We've invited a guitar player who is
  _____ in Mexico. He'll
  4 (among / great)
  play _____ Mexican guitar
  5 (some / famous)
  songs for you to enjoy.
- You'll see _____ French
  6 (one / funny)
  puppet shows ever!
- There will be an exhibit of wonderful paintings
  by _____ professional
  7 (one / young)
  artists in Brazil.

It's going to be _____ festivals of the summer!
8 (one / amazing)

GRAMMAR PRACTICE **131**

A Complete the conversation about a new TV show. Use *isn't*, *wasn't*, *weren't*, or *didn't*.

Lars: Emma, _____didn't_____ you love the first episode of *Good-bye, San Diego* last night?
                    1

Emma: Yes! _____ San Diego a beautiful city?
                 2

Lars: It certainly is. _____ it a great idea to film the first episode outdoors?
                           3

Emma: I agree. And _____ James Fields a great actor?
                        4

Lars: Yes, he is! But _____ you think the entire cast did a great job?
                          5

Emma: Yes, I did. _____ you surprised last month when they announced Fields was
                       6
going to play the main character?

Lars: I sure was! And _____ he ask for a million dollars just for one season?
                           7

Emma: Yes, and he got it!

B Read the statements. Then rewrite them as negative questions for a TV star.

1. You are tired of being interviewed all the time.
   Aren't you tired of being interviewed all the time?

2. It is hard to be a minor character in two TV series at the same time.
   _____

3. You felt that one series was enough.
   _____

4. It was difficult to convince your bosses that you could manage it.
   _____

5. You were surprised when both shows became big successes.
   _____

6. You are excited about next month's season finales.
   _____

7. You are angry at cast members who have shared spoilers about them.
   _____

8. You hope that both shows will want you back next year.
   _____

C MAKE IT PERSONAL Imagine you want to know a friend's opinions of TV shows or
TV watching habits. Write negative questions.

1. _Weren't you glad that The Speed of Light was continued for another season?_
2. _____
3. _____
4. _____
5. _____

UNIT 3, LESSON 3 ADVERBIAL INTENSIFIERS WITH ADJECTIVES

A Rewrite the sentences using the adverb in parentheses.

1. That app is useful. (incredibly)
   That app is incredibly useful.

2. This restaurant is crowded tonight. (unusually)
   _____

3. You missed out on a good meeting. (surprisingly)
   _____

4. I'm reading an interesting book. (really)
   _____

5. It's supposed to be cold tomorrow. (extremely)
   _____

6. The networking event was boring. (utterly)
   _____

B MAKE IT PERSONAL Write sentences about an event you recently attended. Use one word from each box in each sentence.

surprisingly extremely totally utterly amazingly incredibly	good exciting fun boring interesting nice

1. I went to an amazingly good concert last week.
2. _____
3. _____
4. _____

UNIT 3, LESSON 4 VOCABULARY PRACTICE

Read the definitions. Then complete the sentences with the words.

> **a recommendation**: a suggestion or advice about the best thing to do
> **stressful**: causing a lot of worry or nervousness
> **take (something) by storm**: to become very popular over a short period of time
> **an anniversary**: a date on which something happened in a previous year
> **uneventful**: when nothing exciting or interesting happens
> **a producer**: someone who makes a movie or TV show
> **a break**: a short time during which you stop doing something
> **a viewer**: someone who watches a TV show

1. Many _____ of that TV show didn't like the season finale.
2. I can't decide where to go for lunch. Do you have a _____?
3. It's our five-year _____, so we're going out to dinner tonight.
4. My new job is really _____. My boss gives me new projects every week.
5. Nothing special happened this weekend. It was _____ and a little boring.
6. Let's take a _____ from studying and watch a movie.
7. That song has _____ the country _____. I hear it everywhere.
8. That show has gotten much better since the hired a new _____.

A Complete the conversation about online shopping. Use the clauses and phrases in the box.

how to use it	where to buy	who I'm shopping	why you closed
what you're doing	where it says	~~where you went~~	why they're so

Lela: Oh, here you are…on the computer! I didn't know __where you went__ .
         1

Mom: Oh, hi, Lela. I'm just doing a little online shopping.

Lela: I don't understand _____ the door. What's the big secret?
                              2

Mom: Can't you guess _____ for?
                          3

Lela: Oh! You're shopping for Dad and don't want him to know _____ .
                                                                  4

Mom: That's right. I'm shopping for a jacket for him. I don't know

         _____ expensive.
              5

Lela: Have you decided _____ the jacket from?
                            6

Mom: Jacket World, I guess. I received a coupon code, but I don't know _____ .
                                                                          7

Lela: It's easy. Just type it in the box _____ "coupon code." You get free
                                             8
         shipping, too, so it'll be here just in time for Dad's birthday!

B Read the scrambled sentences from a conversation between a store clerk and a customer. Then reorder the words to make questions and statements.

1. what / know / is? / it / size / you / Do
   Do you know what size it is?

2. are / why / tell / returning this item? / me / you / Could you

   _____

3. put / you / Do / know / the / where / receipt? / you

   _____

4. how much / paid / you / Do / remember / it? / you / for

   _____

5. a / how / tell / to / get / me / store card. / Please

   _____

6. give / you / I don't / cash. / understand / why / can't / me

   _____

C MAKE IT PERSONAL Imagine you are shopping. Complete the *wh-* clauses and phrases to make polite requests and ask indirect questions.

1. Do you know what this store sells on its website _____ ?
2. Do you remember where _____ ?
3. Please tell me when _____ .
4. Can you explain why _____ ?
5. Could you tell me how _____ ?

UNIT 4, LESSON 2   *THINK, IMAGINE,* AND *WONDER* FOR REQUESTS

A Complete the conversation between a customer and a sales clerk. Use the words and phrases in the box.

could	I imagine	I wonder	that	if
imagine	~~I wonder if~~	think you		

Customer: ___I wonder if___ you could help me. I'd like to return
                                    1
this sweater.

Clerk: Of course. Do you _____ could tell me the problem?
                                           2

Customer: It's defective. _____ you can help me, right?
                                     3

Clerk: Well, first, do you think _____ you could tell me how it's defective?
                                              4

Customer: Let me show you. Look at this. _____ if you can see the problem.
                                                        5

Clerk: Oh, I do see. I _____ you can't wear it with a broken zipper.
                                  6

Customer: No, of course not. Do you think I _____ exchange it?
                                                           7

Clerk: Sure. I wonder _____ you could wait here for just a moment.
                                  8

B Read the customer requests. Then rewrite and soften them, using the verbs in parentheses.

1. Could I return this shirt? (think)
   <u>Do you think that I could return this shirt?</u>
2. Could you explain your return policy? (wonder)
   _____
3. Can I try this on in the dressing room? (imagine)
   _____
4. Could you order me a pair of these shoes? (think)
   _____
5. Could I return this sweater? (wonder)
   _____
6. Can I use my store credit to buy this? (imagine)
   _____
7. Could I have these things delivered to my home? (think)
   _____

C MAKE IT PERSONAL Imagine you are talking to a store clerk. Complete the requests.

1. Do you think I could <u>speak to the manager</u> _____?
2. Do you think you could _____?
3. I wonder if I could _____.
4. I imagine you could _____.
5. I wonder if you could _____.
6. I imagine I can _____.

UNIT 4, LESSON 3   *WHILE* AND *WHEREAS*

Ⓐ Complete the sentences. Use the clauses in the box.

> whereas there is no extra charge   while I prefer small stores   ~~it has very few books~~
> it doesn't sell furniture   whereas his wife wants to wait   Amy prefers to shop alone

1. While this bookstore has a great selection of music, _it has very few books_____.
2. There's a processing fee to purchase tickets online, _____
   for ticket sales in person.
3. My sister loves big shopping malls, _____.
4. Whereas Claire always goes shopping with her friends,
   _____.
5. John wants to buy an expensive TV right away, _____
   until they find a better deal.
6. While that store sells small items for the home, _____.

Ⓑ **MAKE IT PERSONAL** Complete the sentences by adding a clause with *while* or *whereas*.
Use commas as needed.

1. Some people shop for specific brands _, while others look for the best deal_____.
2. Video games are on sale this week _____.
3. Some stores offer free delivery _____.
4. I rarely purchase furniture online _____.

UNIT 4, LESSON 4 VOCABULARY PRACTICE

Read the definitions. Then complete the sentences with the words.

> **a possession**: something that you have or own
> **identity**: who or what you are
> **remind (someone) of**: to make someone remember something
> **an heirloom**: a valuable object that has belonged to the same family for many years
> **have sentimental value**: to be connected to feelings and memories, not to money
> **a substitute**: a person or thing that takes the place of another person or thing
> **pass away**: to die
> **associate**: to make a connection between things or people in your mind

1. Do you have any family _____ that you will give to your children?
2. A short email is not a _____ for a personal, handwritten letter.
3. This old book isn't an expensive antique, but it has _____ because my
   uncle gave it to me.
4. You _____ my best friend because you have the same hair and
   eye color.
5. I don't have many _____. I like to live very simply.
6. Her volunteer work with children is a big part of her _____.
7. My cat _____ yesterday, and I'm very sad.

UNIT 5, LESSON 1   PAST INTENTIONS

A Complete the conversation about past intentions. Use the infinitive or gerund form of the verbs in parentheses.

David: You look a little down, Tanya. Is anything the matter?

Tanya: Not really. It's just that I was hoping ___to make___ so
1 (make)
many healthy changes in my life, but I haven't had any
success yet. For example, I was going _____ more
2 (get)
exercise, but the gym near my house closed down. And I
was planning on _____ healthier food, but I never have time to cook.
3 (eat)

David: I know what you mean! I was hoping _____ time in nature during
4 (spend)
my vacation, but my family wanted to go to Chicago. And I was planning on
_____ meditation, but it was kind of boring.
5 (practice)

Tanya: Healthy habits are important, but they can be difficult. I was thinking about
_____ more water, but I really need my coffee!
6 (drink)

David: I was planning _____ eating out, but that's impossible.
7 (stop)

Tanya: Why is that impossible?

David: Because I don't like the taste of my own cooking!

B Complete the sentences about health resolutions that a family did not keep. Use the past continuous and the gerund or infinitive forms of the words in parentheses.

1. We ___were going to join___ a yoga class together, but it was canceled.
(go, join)
2. Our son _____ coffee, but he couldn't get up without it.
(plan on, give up)
3. Our daughter _____ early to exercise, but she hasn't yet.
(think about, get up)
4. We _____ bicycles for the whole family, but they were too expensive.
(go, buy)
5. We _____ the summer in the mountains, but our daughter got sick.
(hope, spend)
6. We _____ out of the city, but the country might be too quiet for us.
(think about, move)
7. We _____ regular medical checkups, but we've been very busy lately.
(plan on, get)

C MAKE IT PERSONAL Complete the sentences. Use past intentions that are true for you.

1. I was going ___to get up early this morning,___ but ___my alarm clock didn't ring___.
2. I was planning on _____ but _____.
3. I was hoping _____ but _____.
4. I was planning _____ but _____.
5. I was thinking about _____ but _____.

A Complete the conversation about soccer. Use the sentences in the box.

I am, too	I haven't either	Neither did I	So do I
I did, too	I wasn't either	Neither could I	~~So did I~~

Tony: I had a great time playing soccer yesterday.

Onur: ___So did I___ ! I didn't play very well, though.
    1

Tony: _____ . I wasn't moving very well on the field.
        2

Onur: _____ . And I couldn't control the ball very well.
        3

Tony: _____ . I wish I had more time to practice.
        4

Onur: _____ . I'm really sore today.
        5

Tony: _____ . I think I pulled a muscle in my back.
        6

Onur: I think _____ . I've never done that before.
            7

Tony: _____ . I hope we're not getting too old to play soccer!
        8

B Complete the text message conversation about tennis. Use the correct auxiliary verb and *so, too, neither,* or *either.*

I'm planning on joining the town tennis club.

Really? I didn't know the town had a tennis club.

___Neither did___ I. I just saw it last week.
    1
But I haven't played tennis in years.

I _____ . Back in high school,
    2
I was on the school tennis team.

I _____ , for a little while, but
    3
I had to stop because I hurt my arm.

Really? I _____ ! But I'd
            4
really like to start playing again.

_____ I. I'm not getting enough exercise lately.
    5

_____ I. But to be honest,
        6
I can't play tennis very well anymore.

I _____ , but I think it would be fun to play together!
    7

C MAKE IT PERSONAL Read the replies. Write statements about health, symptoms, or injuries that are true for you.

1. **A:** _I don't get sick very often._   **B:** Neither do I.
2. **A:** _____   **B:** So do I.
3. **A:** _____   **B:** I have, too.
4. **A:** _____   **B:** I wouldn't either.

UNIT 5, LESSON 3 PLANS AND INTENTIONS FOR THE FUTURE

A Use the words to make sentences about future plans and intentions.

1. Hannah / intend / get / more exercise.
   <u>Hannah intends to get more exercise.</u>

2. Jack / plan / see / a doctor soon.
   _____

3. I / mean / wake up / early tomorrow.
   _____

4. We / not intend / stay up / late tonight.
   _____

5. Lee / not plan / work / tomorrow.
   _____

6. you / intend / take / a nap this afternoon?
   _____

B MAKE IT PERSONAL Write sentences about your plans to stay healthy. Use *intend*, *mean*, or *plan* + infinitive.

1. <u>I intend to eat healthier breakfasts.</u>
2. _____
3. _____
4. _____

UNIT 5, LESSON 4 VOCABULARY PRACTICE

Read the definitions. Then complete the sentences with the words.

> **peak performance:** the very best an athlete can do
> **endurance:** the ability to continue doing something difficult over a long period of time
> **vary:** be different
> **a positive attitude:** good opinions and feelings about something
> **a means to an end:** something that you do to achieve a result, not because you want to
> **a commitment:** the hard work and loyalty someone gives to an activity

1. Exercise routines _____ from person to person.
2. Long-distance swimming requires a lot of _____.
3. She practices for so many hours. You can really see her _____ to improving.
4. This job is just _____. I'm trying to save money for a new car.
5. He was at _____ in his final game last year, but he hasn't been as good this year.
6. Ken's _____ puts everyone on the team in a better mood.

A Complete the article about a robbery. Use the past perfect form of the verbs in parentheses.

ROBBERY AT THE CENTRAL DEPARTMENT STORE

Thieves broke into the Central Department Store yesterday after it __had closed__ for the day. The alarm did not go
1 (close)
off because the thieves _____ the electricity
2 (turn off)
before breaking in. The store security guard was working, but he _____ asleep in a chair. The thieves tied
3 (fall)
him up with some rope that they _____ with
4 (bring)
them. Later, the guard noticed that the thieves _____ his hands very well, and he was
5 (not tie)
able to escape. However, he couldn't call the police because they _____ his phone away
6 (take)
from him. He ran as fast as he could out of the store and to the police station. When the thieves
noticed that he _____, they were afraid he would bring the police, so they decided not
7 (escaped)
to rob the store after all. By the time the police arrived, the thieves _____. The police
8 (leave)
interviewed people nearby, but they _____ anything. If you have any information that
9 (not see)
might help find these thieves, contact the police immediately.

B Complete the sentences. Use the verbs in parentheses. Use the simple past and the past perfect once each in each sentence.

1. Although the taxi driver ___had said___ $20 at the airport, he ___asked___ me for $50
   (said)   **(ask)**
   when we arrived in the city.

2. I left my laptop on the restaurant table while I went to the bathroom, and by the time
   I _____, someone _____ it!
   (return)   **(steal)**

3. I _____ my wallet in my shoe before I _____ swimming, but while
   (hide)   **(go)**
   I was in the water, a thief found it and stole all the money and credit cards.

4. I'm so glad that I _____ my cell phone in my handbag before the thief
   (not put)
   _____ it.
   (steal)

5. The sales clerk was very friendly, but when I _____ my money later, I realized
   (count)
   that he _____ me enough change.
   (not give)

C MAKE IT PERSONAL Imagine you traveled to a new city. Complete the sentences with the past perfect.

1. I felt safe because _I had chosen to stay in a five-star hotel_____.
2. When I returned to my hotel room, I noticed that someone _____.
3. The thief couldn't find my money because I _____.
4. I knew where to find nice gifts to buy because I _____.
5. After I left the restaurant, I realized that I _____.
6. I was worried while I was walking because _____.
7. When I saw my hotel bill, I was glad that I _____.

UNIT 6, LESSON 2   PRESENT PERFECT PASSIVE

A Complete the conversation between two police detectives. Use the present perfect passive form of the verbs in parentheses.

A: _____Has_____ any progress __been made__ in the Patterson
1 (make)
murder case yet?

B: Oh, yes. A lot. Two new witnesses who saw the murder

_____. An excellent drawing of the suspect
2 (find)
_____ by the police artist, and copies
3 (make)
_____ already _____ to newspapers and
4 (send)
television stations.

A: Excellent! And _____ a telephone line _____
5 (set up)
yet for people to call if they see him?

B: Yes, one has, and a lot of useful information _____ already _____.
6 (collect)
It seems that the suspect _____ more than once in the city.
7 (see)

A: Very good! By the way, _____ the airport police _____ to watch out
8 (tell)
for him yet?

B: Yes, they have. We should arrest him soon.

B Rewrite the sentences using the present perfect passive. Use a *by* phrase if appropriate.

1. Have the police contacted the victim's family yet?
   Has the victim's family been contacted by the police yet?

2. The police have already interviewed two witnesses.
   _____

3. The detective hasn't arrested the suspect yet.
   _____

4. Has the doctor examined the body of the victim yet?
   _____

5. A crowd of people has surrounded the scene.
   _____

6. The suspect has already hired a lawyer.
   _____

7. Have the police found the murder weapon yet?
   _____

C MAKE IT PERSONAL Imagine your house or apartment has been robbed. What do you notice? Write sentences using the present perfect passive.

1. The living room window has been broken.
2. _____
3. _____
4. _____
5. _____

A Complete the sentences using *do, don't, does, doesn't, did,* or *didn't.*

1. The lines on your hand change over time, but your fingerprints ____don't____.
2. The police didn't find any bloodstains, but the forensic investigator _____.
3. An open wound bleeds, but a bruise usually _____.
4. The DNA showed the criminal's ethnic background, but the fingerprints _____.
5. Not all crime scenes contain DNA evidence, but many of them _____.
6. Fifty years ago the government didn't have a DNA database, but now it _____.

B MAKE IT PERSONAL Complete the sentences by adding a contrasting idea. Use *do, don't,* or *did* to replace verbs instead of repeating them.

1. On TV, fingerprints usually lead police to a criminal, but _____in real life, they don't_____.
2. Some forensic scientists work for the police department, but _____.
3. Lawyers don't analyze forensic evidence, _____.
4. My neighbor didn't witness the crime, _____.

UNIT 6, LESSON 4 VOCABULARY PRACTICE

Read the definitions. Then complete the sentences with the words.

> **figure out:** to understand something after thinking about it
> **catch red-handed:** to catch someone while the person is doing something bad
> **accuse:** to say that someone has done something wrong or illegal
> **a technique:** a special way of doing something
> **analysis:** careful examination of something in order to understand it
> **influence:** to have an effect on the way someone or something develops, behaves, or thinks
> **preserve:** to keep something from being destroyed or changed too much
> **rigorous:** careful and making sure nothing is missed

1. The detective was fired because his work was not _____ enough.
2. The assistant _____ her boss of stealing the company's money.
3. Forensic scientists performed a careful _____ of the crime scene.
4. I have thought and thought about it, but I just can't _____ the answer.
5. The thieves were _____ in the house they were burglarizing.
6. They are keeping people away from the crime scene to _____ it for the investigators.
7. My parents _____ me in many ways, including how I see the world.
8. She learned her interviewing _____ from a famous detective.

A Read the conversation from a party. Cross out the correct words to create reduced defining relative clauses.

Jenna: Where is the young man ~~who was~~ carrying that plate of appetizers? I'm ready for
₁
another one.

Dan: I am, too. Those were delicious appetizers. Who made them?

Jenna: I think the boss's wife did. **She's the woman that is standing next to the piano.**
₂

Dan: **Do you mean the one who is wearing the green sweater?**
₃

Jenna: No. She's on the other side. **She's the one who is wearing the floral skirt.**
₄

Dan: Oh, I see her now. **And who are the guys that are talking with her?**
₅

Jenna: Those are her sons. They were serving, but it looks like they've finished now.

Dan: The appetizers are probably gone then. **I think that group of people who are sitting**
₆
near the kitchen door ate most of them, especially the tall guy who's wearing the
₇
tight jacket.

Jenna: **Do you mean the handsome one that's looking this way?** That's my husband!
₈

B Read the statements made by a shopping center security guard. Rewrite each set as a single statement. Make the second sentence a reduced defining relative clause.

1. I'm going to talk to the woman. She's dropping clothes on the floor.
   <u>I'm going to talk to the woman dropping clothes on the floor.</u>

2. I don't recognize those boys. They are trying on baseball caps.
   _____

3. I've never seen that guy. He is waiting for the elevator.
   _____

4. That woman is another security guard. She is waving at me.
   _____

5. I see two regular customers. They are talking to the manager.
   _____

6. I just heard a store alarm. It was going off for some reason.
   _____

7. I think I see a guy. He is stealing a shirt!
   _____

C MAKE IT PERSONAL Imagine you are on a train. Complete the sentences with reduced defining relative clauses to describe people around you.

1. That woman <u>collecting tickets from the passengers</u> is the conductor.
2. The woman _____ is a company president.
3. The man and woman _____ are probably tourists.
4. The children _____ are bothering the other riders.
5. The man _____ just realized he missed his stop.

UNIT 7, LESSON 2   PASSIVE CAUSATIVES

A Read each statement about old clothes and then complete the reply. Use the causative with the verbs in parentheses and a pronoun.

1. A: The sleeves on this coat are too short.
   B: Why don't you __have them lengthened__ ?
   (have, lengthen)
2. A: I really like this jacket, but the zipper's broken.
   B: You should _____ .
   (get, replace)
3. A: I'd like to wear this suit to the wedding, but it's really dirty.
   B: I think there's still time to _____ .
   (get, dry clean)
4. A: My brother gave me these pants, but they're too long for me.
   B: How expensive would it be to _____ ?
   (have, hem)
5. A: I've lost so much weight that these pants are too loose for me now.
   B: You need to _____ . I know a tailor who can do it for you.
   (get, take in)
6. A: Do these pants look like they fit me, or are they too tight?
   B: They're too tight. If you want to wear them, you need to _____ .
   (have, let out)
7. A: Should I keep these damaged shoes or throw them away?
   B: Throw them away. It would be too expensive to _____ .
   (get, repair)
8. A: I'd like to give these old clothes to a charity, but I don't know where to take them.
   B: You can _____ from your house if you call this number.
   (have, pick up)

B Igor just bought an old house that needs a lot of work, but he can't do the work himself. Rewrite the tasks using the passive causative.

1. He needs to check the heating system.
   He needs to have the heating system checked.
2. He needs to cut the grass.
3. He wants to replace the windows.
4. He is planning to paint the house.
5. He is going to put in a pool.
6. He wants to build a garage.

C MAKE IT PERSONAL Imagine you are staying in a hotel. Use the passive causative to ask for things you need the staff to do for you.

1. I need to have breakfast served in my room tomorrow morning.
2.
3.
4.
5.

A Complete the sentences with *would rather* and a phrase from the box.

not have it dry cleaned	take the bus	wear a suit
be comfortable	~~stay home~~	not negotiate

1. I'm going out with my friends tonight, but I'm really tired. Honestly, I _would rather stay home_____ .
2. My manager is very formal. He _____ than casual clothing to work.
3. Jane doesn't usually drive to work. She _____ so that she can catch up on email on her way.
4. These shoes are pretty, but they hurt my feet. I'm going to wear a different pair of shoes because I _____ .
5. Henry plans to buy a car online. He doesn't want to buy it in person because he _____ the price.
6. Do you think I can wash this jacket at home? I _____ because that's expensive.

B MAKE IT PERSONAL Write sentences about your preferences for a work environment. Use *would rather*.

1. _I would rather work for a small company than a large one._____
2. _____
3. _____
4. _____

UNIT 7, LESSON 4 VOCABULARY PRACTICE

Read the definitions. Then complete the sentences with the words.

a bridal gown: the dress a bride wears at her wedding
fabric: cloth
a ritual: a set of actions that people always do in the same way
specialize (in): to deal with one particular thing so that you know a lot about it
decorative: pretty and used to make something more attractive
a rough sketch: a quick drawing with very little detail
a fitting room: a room for trying on clothes

1. Her shirt has _____ flowers along the collar.
2. She had her _____ made by a famous designer.
3. My morning _____ is to exercise, make coffee, and then read the news.
4. Her dress is made from a beautiful red _____ .
5. The designer drew a _____ so I could see what the suit would look like.
6. They can make anything, but they _____ men's suits.
7. Excuse me, where's the _____ ? I want to try on these pants.

A Complete the conversation about computer problems. Use *wish* or *only* and the phrases in the box.

I had written	I hadn't opened	this hadn't happened	you had installed
I had listened	I had remembered	I hadn't received	he hadn't invited

Mario: I can't believe this. I have to turn in my paper to my professor today, and my laptop won't work. I __wish I hadn't received__ that strange email attachment. ₁

Stacey: I told you to get virus protection software. If _____ some on your computer! ₂

Mario: You're right. I _____ to you. But it's too ₃ late now. Oh, if _____ that attachment! ₄ The sad thing is that I had planned to finish this paper and send it to the professor yesterday, but there was a party at Jin's place. If _____ me! ₅

Stacey: This isn't Jin's fault. Do you have another copy of your paper somewhere?

Mario: The only copy is on this computer. I _____ to save another ₆ copy somewhere! And today's Sunday! The computer repair store is closed today. I _____ on the weekend! ₇

Stacey: Well, what are you going to do now?

Mario: I guess I'll have to talk to the professor. I hate computers! If _____ my paper the old-fashioned way—with a pen! ₈

B Complete the sentences about regrets with *wish* or *only* and the past perfect form of the verbs in parentheses.

1. I _____wish_____ I _____had attended_____ a better college. (**attend**)
2. I _____ I _____ more computer courses. (**take**)
3. I _____ I _____ more about hardware. (**learn**)
4. If _____ my teachers _____ stricter with me. (**be**)
5. My parents _____ my education _____ them so much money. (**not cost**)
6. If _____ I _____ how to type faster. (**know**)

C MAKE IT PERSONAL Think about five of your regrets in the areas below. Complete the sentences so they are true for you.

1. Language learning: I wish I had _used social media to practice speaking English._
2. Language learning: I wish I had / hadn't _____ when I was younger.
3. Technology: If only I had / hadn't _____ when I was younger.
4. Money: I wish I had / hadn't _____ when I was younger.
5. School: If only I had / hadn't _____ when I was younger.

UNIT 8, LESSON 2 SHOWING PURPOSE

A Complete the conversation about a new phone. Write *for* or *to*.

A: Look at all the cool apps you have! What does this one do?

B: I use that one _____to_____ get maps and driving directions.
1

A: What about that one with the television icon?

B: That's an app I use _____ watch TV shows.
2

A: Really? I think that phone is too small to use _____ watching TV.
3

B: Actually, it's not bad. And it doesn't cost anything _____ use the service.
4

A: That's good. This green icon looks interesting.

B: I use that _____ business all the time.
5

A: What does it do?

B: It opens an app that I use _____ having big phone meetings.
6

A: That sounds cool! I can only use my phone _____ speak to one person at a
7
time. Where can I go _____ download that app?
8

B: I'll check. What are you going to use it for? Business?

A: No. I just miss my family, and I think it would be fun _____ talk to everyone at
9
the same time!

B Write *in order to* or *for* to complete the list of guidelines for new office employees.

1. Please don't use your private phone _____in order to_____ make business calls.
2. These guidelines are very important _____ all employees to read.
3. You need to create a password _____ access the company network.
4. Click the green arrow icon _____ upload files to the company website.
5. Use the red arrow icon _____ downloading files from the website.
6. Never use the company email service _____ sending private emails.
7. Please use the MeetingPlan software _____ reserve a meeting room.
8. You can always call the computer center _____ report any problems.
9. Contact Sasha in technical support _____ more information on company technology policies.

C MAKE IT PERSONAL Complete the sentences so they are true for you.

1. I have used search engines to _____find information about famous people_____.
2. I have used apps for _____.
3. I have gone online many times in order to _____.
4. I have often texted friends to _____.
5. I have downloaded software for _____.
6. I have used a laptop in order to _____.

UNIT 8, LESSON 3 *EVEN* TO EMPHASIZE A POINT

A Rewrite the second sentence in each pair using *even* to emphasize the point.

1. Jack knows nothing about social media. He doesn't have a social media account.
   <u>He doesn't even have a social media account.</u>

2. I didn't get Ava a birthday card. I didn't remember that it was her birthday.
   _____

3. No one did well on the test. Dan did badly, and he's an excellent student.
   _____

4. Michael lost touch with everyone. He hasn't stayed in touch with his best friend.
   _____

5. Lily didn't want to work for her father's company. She didn't consider it.
   _____

6. You can't check your social media on that computer. It isn't connected.
   _____

B MAKE IT PERSONAL Write sentences about how you use social media to connect with friends and family. Use *even* to stress an idea or emphasize a point.

1. <u>I don't go even one day without connecting with my friends online.</u>
2. _____
3. _____
4. _____

UNIT 8, LESSON 4 VOCABULARY PRACTICE

Read the definitions. Then complete the sentences with the words.

> **a structure:** something that has been built
> **efficient:** working well, in a way that does not waste time, money, or energy
> **modular:** made from separate parts that can be put together
> **revolutionary:** completely new and different in a way that leads to great improvements
> **a resident:** someone who lives in a particular place
> **an alternative:** something that can be done or used instead of something else
> **a pedestrian:** a person who is walking along a street or sidewalk
> **a sensor:** a piece of equipment used to find light, heat, or movement
> **monitor:** to carefully watch something to see if it changes
> **unique:** not like anything else

1. This building is completely _____. You won't find another one like it anywhere.
2. The light has a motion _____. It saves energy, so it's very _____.
3. The walls and ceiling of this _____ were built beforehand. It's a _____ home.
4. The city needs to _____ how much water people are using.
5. He thinks his ideas are _____, but I've heard them all before.
6. The driver stopped to let the _____ cross the street.
7. He has been a _____ of this city for over ten years.
8. I don't like my internet company. I wonder if there's any _____.

UNIT 9, LESSON 1   CAUSATIVE VERBS: *GET, HAVE,* AND *MAKE*

A Complete the conversation between two staff members at a conference. Use the base or infinitive form of the verbs in parentheses.

A: I can't get the security officer ____to open____ the conference room
   1 (open)

doors. We can't make the presenters _____ in the lobby!
                                       2 (wait)

B: Relax. I'll call his supervisor. She'll make him _____ .
                                                    3 (listen)

A: That's great. And after the doors are open, I'll get the tech support

team _____ the video equipment.
      4 (prepare)

B: By the way, there are only a few conference schedules left. We'll definitely need more.

A: OK, I will have someone _____ some more copies. Did you speak to
                            5 (make)

the caterer?

B: Oh, yes, I did. I got him _____ the coffee stand in the lobby open all day.
                             6 (keep)

A: OK. I got Tanya _____ to be the greeter today, but she's sick.
                   7 (agree)

B: Wow. Well, if you can't get someone else _____ it, then I guess I'll have to.
                                              8 (do)

A: But you're the conference manager. We can't make you _____ as the greeter!
                                                         9 (work)

B Rewrite the sentences using the causative verbs in parentheses.

1. The receptionist reserved the meeting room. (have)
   We _had the receptionist reserve the meeting room._

2. The maintenance staff cleaned the meeting room. (have)
   We _____

3. The tech support team connected our laptops to the network. (get)
   We _____

4. Yusuf from accounting spoke first. (make)
   We _____

5. Keiko from sales took the meeting notes. (have)
   We _____

6. A caterer brought in lunch. (get)
   We _____

C MAKE IT PERSONAL Remember six things that you had others do or that others had you do for them. Write sentences using the causative verbs in parentheses.

Home:
1. (make) _My mother made me cut the grass every week._
2. (have) _____
3. (get) _____

School:
1. (make) _____
2. (have) _____
3. (get) _____

UNIT 9, LESSON 2   ADVICE, OBLIGATION, AND EXPECTATION

A Complete the conversation about an important business deal. Use *have*, *has*, *supposed*, or *better*.

Nikki: John, do you _____have_____ to leave immediately?
1

John: Well, I'm _____ to go to a meeting, but it's OK if I'm late.
2

Nikki: Great. You had _____ close the door. I _____ to
3   4
thank you for your help in the negotiations today. If all goes well,
we're hoping to do something for you.

John: You mean a promotion? A raise?

Nikki: I had _____ not say until I show the CEO those signed contracts.
5

John: Signed? Was the client _____ to sign them today?
6

Nikki: Of course. He _____ to sign them or there's no deal.
7

John: Well, he didn't! And he's _____ to catch a flight to New York in one hour!
8
Come on–let's go to the airport!

B Complete the conversation about buying a house. Use the words in the box.

better	don't have	have	~~have to~~
better not	has to	have to	not supposed

Roger: My wife and I really like the car you're selling. Can I talk to you about that?

Seller: Well, I _____have to_____ meet another couple that's interested in the car soon. If you're
1
interested, you had _____ wait too long to make a decision.
2

Roger: I know, but I'm _____ to make a decision without my wife. She
3
_____ stay home with the kids all day. They've got the flu.
4

Seller: Look, I'll take 10 percent off the price. I _____ to do this, but I like you.
5
But you _____ to sign the contract now.
6

Roger: Wow, that's really nice of you. But I had _____ call my wife first.
7

Seller: OK, but if you want the deal, you _____ make a decision soon.
8

C MAKE IT PERSONAL Complete the sentences with your advice.

1. When you need new furniture, you don't always have to _buy it from a furniture store_ .
2. If you want to get a good price on a car, you have to _____ .
3. Before you sign any contract, you're supposed to _____ .
4. During price negotiations, you're not supposed to _____ .
5. If you're planning to buy a house, you'd better _____ .

A Rewrite the sentence to change *if...not* to *unless*.

1. I can't help you if you don't pay attention.
   <u>I can't help you unless you pay attention.</u>

2. If we don't make an effort, we'll never finish this project.
   _____

3. You'll be late for your interview if you don't hurry.
   _____

4. We won't meet again this week if you don't have questions.
   _____

5. If they can't offer a higher salary, I will reject their job offer.
   _____

6. Don't sign that contract if you haven't read it.
   _____

B MAKE IT PERSONAL Complete the sentences using phrases with *unless*.

1. <u>Unless you propose a new idea</u>_____, we will stick to the original plan.
2. _____, we won't know where to go.
3. _____, I probably won't get a promotion.
4. _____, I won't do well in a negotiation.

UNIT 9, LESSON 4 VOCABULARY PRACTICE

Read the definitions. Then complete the sentences with the words.

> **broad:** including a large number of people or things
> **a party:** one of the people involved in an argument or discussion
> **a middle ground:** an area of agreement between two opposite sides
> **a position:** someone's opinion about something
> **on track:** likely to lead to a success or the correct result
> **establish:** to start a relationship, an organization or a business
> **partially:** not completely

1. We need to keep this meeting _____ so we can finish on time.
2. Don't just think about what you want from the negotiation. Ask what the other _____ wants as well.
3. We will learn a lot of details in this class, but the _____ topic is negotiating.
4. Start out with some personal conversation to try to _____ a good relationship.
5. They walked away from the negotiation because they couldn't find a _____.
6. We weren't excited about the result, but at least we were _____ satisfied.
7. What is your _____ on the new rule? Are you for or against it?

A Complete the meeting notes. Use the phrases in the box.

| if we wanted   us whether we   whether she was   if she had |
| if we were   me whether I   ~~whether I could~~ |

- Michael asked me <u>whether I could</u> take the meeting notes. I agreed.
  ₁
- Leo asked us _____ coffee. We said yes, and he brought some in.
  ₂
- Hector asked _____ were ready to start. Everyone said yes.
  ₃
- Kimiko asked _____ happy with the new office. Most people said yes.
  ₄
- I asked Lisa _____ writing the annual report. Lisa said it would be finished soon.
  ₅
- Hector asked Donna _____ any suggestions about how to increase profits.
  ₆
- Donna asked _____ could email my meeting notes to the group. I told her I would.
  ₇

B Read the direct questions from an interview. Then complete the reported questions.

1. Can you tell me about yourself?
   She asked me if <u>I could tell her about myself</u>.
2. Do you have a driver's license?
   She asked me whether _____.
3. Are you a college graduate?
   She asked me if _____.
4. Can you speak any foreign languages?
   She asked me whether _____.
5. Are you interested in a management position?
   She asked me if _____.
6. Do you have any questions for me?
   She asked me whether _____.
7. Can you start immediately?
   She asked me if _____.

C MAKE IT PERSONAL Complete the embedded questions. Use information that is true for you.

1. My teacher asked me if <u>I had finished my homework</u>.
2. My classmate asked me whether _____.
3. A friend of mine asked me if _____.
4. _____ asked me whether _____.
5. _____ asked me if _____.

A Complete the conversation between co-workers. Use the correct prepositions. More than one correct answer may be possible.

Arthur: What are you looking _____for_____, Diana?

1

Diana: My bottle of aspirin. I just got out of a terrible meeting.

Arthur: I'm sorry to hear that. Who were you meeting _____?

2

Diana: Lisa, Victor, Leo, and some clients.

Arthur: What were you talking _____?

3

Diana: The clients' advertising plans. I didn't like some of the ideas.

Arthur: I see. Who did you disagree _____?

4

Diana: Leo.

Arthur: Which department does he work _____?

5

Diana: Accounting. He is against spending more money, but I think we need to.

Arthur: I see. What should we spend more money _____?

6

Diana: Well, better graphics. But it's not Leo who made me angry.

Arthur: Really? Who are you angry _____?

7

Diana: A couple of the clients. While I was talking to Leo, they started laughing.

Arthur: What were they laughing _____?

8

Diana: They were looking at some silly website on their phones instead of listening.

B Read the statements about people in an office. Write questions with final prepositions to get more information.

1. Emilia is upset about something that happened. <u>What is she upset about</u> ?
2. Christopher usually disagrees with someone. _____ ?
3. Amanda ran into somebody at lunch. _____ ?
4. Pietro is laughing about something. _____ ?
5. I'm taking care of something very important. _____ ?
6. We always laughed at one person in meetings. _____ ?
7. The security guards are looking for something. _____ ?

C MAKE IT PERSONAL Read the sentences. Write a question with a final preposition that you could ask this person.

1. A friend has just finished a class. <u>What did the teacher talk about?</u>
2. A friend just finished a telephone call. _____
3. A friend is in a very bad mood. _____
4. A friend isn't paying attention in class. _____
5. A friend says he or she has a lot of money. _____

A Use the words in the box to complete the sentences with a repeated comparative.

| dark | ~~demanding~~ | expensive | good | hungry | large |

1. Helen has several new responsibilities at work. Her job is getting
   _____more and more demanding_____.
2. I hope we're going to eat soon. I'm getting _____.
3. Our sales team is getting _____. We started out with only
   four sales representatives, but now we have over twenty.
4. I think it will rain soon. The sky is becoming _____.
5. I can't believe how much this phone costs! Phones are becoming
   _____.
6. Alec and Jake used to argue a lot, but now they're getting along
   _____.

B MAKE IT PERSONAL Complete the sentences with parallel comparatives.

1. The older I get, _____the wiser I become_____.
2. The less I study, _____.
3. The more you practice, _____.
4. The more people talk, _____.

UNIT 10, LESSON 4 VOCABULARY PRACTICE

Read the definitions. Then complete the sentences with the words.

> **altruism**: the practice of caring about the needs of others before dealing with your own
> **a donation**: money or items that you give to help others
> **a sacrifice**: something that you decide not to have or do so that something more
>   important can happen
> **constant**: happening all the time
> **humanity**: people in general

1. If we want to have money for a vacation next summer, we need to make some
   _____ during the year.
2. Many studies have found that _____ makes people feel happier. It's nice
   to help others.
3. That boy is in _____ motion. He never sits down!
4. We learn about _____ by studying people from different cultures.
5. Every month, I make a small _____ to a local charity.

UNIT 2, LESSON 1   IMPERATIVES IN REPORTED SPEECH

Use *said*, *told*, and *asked* with an infinitive to report past orders and requests.

Direct speech				Reported speech				
Subject	**Verb**	**Object**	**Imperative**	**Subject**	**Verb**	**Object**	**(*Not*) infinitive**	
I	said,	–	"Arrive on time."	I	**said**	–	**to arrive**	on time.
You			"Don't be late."	You				
She	told	him,		She	**told**	him	**not to be**	late.
					asked	us		

Notes
* Never use a noun or pronoun as an object with *said*.
* Always use a noun or pronoun as an object with *told* and *asked*.
* Never use *ask* with imperatives in direct speech.
* Always use a comma before the imperative in direct speech.

UNIT 2, LESSON 1   VERBS FOR REPORTING WHAT SOMEONE SAYS

Verbs for reporting what someone says						
acknowledge	confirm	forbid	mention	recall	reveal	urge
add	continue	guarantee	note	recommend	rule	warn
admit	convince	hint	notify	record	say	whisper
advise	cry	imply	observe	refuse	scream	write
agree	demand	inform	order	remark	shout	yell
announce	deny	inquire	persuade	remind	state	
answer	describe	insist	predict	repeat	suggest	
argue	direct	instruct	promise	reply	teach	
ask	discuss	invite	propose	request	tell	
confess	explain	maintain	reassure	respond	threaten	

Changes in time words		Changes in place words	
Direct speech	**Reported speech**		
now	then, right then, at that moment		
today	that day		
tomorrow	the next day, the following day	**Direct speech**	**Reported speech**
the day after tomorrow	two days later	here ⟶ there	
yesterday	the day before		
last week	the week before, one week earlier	*Example:*	
last month	the month before, one month earlier	"Can you come **here today**?"	
last year	the year before, one year earlier	he asked	
next week	the following week, one week later	He asked me if I could go **there**	
next month	the following month, one month later	**that day**.	
next year	the following year, one year later		
these days	those days		
this week	that week		
a week (month, year) ago	one week (month, year) earlier		

Restrictive relative clauses define the meaning of nouns. They provide information that is necessary to understand the sentence.

Relative pronoun	Used for	Example
who	people	I know the designer **who** made this jacket.
whom	people	Selena is the woman (**whom**) I met at the fashion show.
that	people and things	The man **that** owns the accessories store is sitting over there. It's one of the few pieces of jewelry (**that**) I wear.
Relative adverb		
when	time	I'll always remember the day **when** my husband gave me this ring.
where	place	The store **where** my cousin works is in London.

Notes
- The relative pronouns *who* and *that* can be the subject or the object of the relative clause.
  Subject: *I know the designer **who made** this jacket.*
  (S) (V)
  Object: *It's one of the few pieces of jewelry **that I wear**.*
  (obj)(S) (V)
- The relative pronoun can be deleted when it is the object of the relative clause.
  *It's one of the few pieces of jewelry (**that**) I wear.*

Use the past continuous with *while* and *when* to show that one action was in progress when a second action occurred.

While / When	Subject 1	Was / Were	Verb + -ing	Subject 2	Simple past verb	
While / When	I	**was**	**waiting** for the bus,	it	**started**	to rain.
	she	**was**	**shopping**,	she	**saw**	David.
	we	**were**	**working**,	the power	**went out**.	

Notes
- The action in the *while / when* clause happened first.
  *While I **was waiting** for the bus, people **gave** me strange looks*
      (happened first)   (happened second)
- The *when / while clause* may appear at the beginning or end of a sentence.
  *While I **was getting** dressed, the baby **woke up**.*
  *The baby **woke up** while I **was getting** dressed.*
- *When / while* clauses are dependent clauses. They must be used with independent clauses:
  *When I **was getting** on the elevator, I **got** some more looks.*
      (dependent clause)   (independent clause)

Use the present perfect to show that something has or hasn't happened at an indefinite time in the past. The present perfect is formed with *have* or *has* + past participle.

Questions			Statements			
Have / Has	Subject	Past participle	Subject	*Have / Has*	*Not*	Past participle
Have	you	**been** to the theater?	I	**have**		**been** to the theater.
Has	she	**seen** the play?	She	**has**		**seen** the play.
Have	they	**taken** a bus tour?	They	**have**	not	**taken** a bus tour.

Notes
- The adverbs *yet* and *already* are often used with the present perfect. Use *yet* in questions and negative statements. Use *already* in affirmative statements.
  *Have you seen the play **yet**? I haven't seen the play **yet**.*
  *She has **already** seen the play.* or *She has seen the play **already**.*
- It is possible to have more than one verb after *have* or *has*.
  It is not necessary to repeat *have* or *has*.
  *I **have traveled** to Paris and **have seen** the Eiffel Tower.*
  More common: *I **have traveled** to Paris and **seen** the Eiffel Tower.*
- Use the simple past when the specific time of the event is mentioned. *I **took** a tour **last week**.*

Use contractions, such as *haven't* or *hasn't*, in spoken English and informal writing.

Use the passive when it is not known or not important who performs an action.

Simple present passive

Subject	*Be*	*(Not)*	Past participle	
I	am		employed	as a director.
The movie	is	(not)	adapted	from a book
Blockbusters	are		released	every day.

Simple past passive

Subject	*Be*	*(Not)*	Past participle	
The movie	was	(not)	filmed	last year.
The actors	were		known	in Hollywood.

Notes

- In passive sentences, the focus shifts from the agent to the object.
  Active: *People invited <u>the writer</u>.*   Passive: *<u>The writer</u> was invited.*
- Use *by* when it *is* important to know who performs an action:
  *The role is played **by** award-winning actor Henry Davis.*
- In questions, the verb *be* comes before the subject:
  ***Are you** employed now?*   *Where **were you** employed last year?*

Use present unreal conditionals to talk about untrue or imagined situations and their results.

Statements

If-clause				Result clause			
If	Subject	Simple past		Subject	*Would / Wouldn't*	Base form of verb	
If	I	were	rich,	I	would	donate	more money.
	she	had	more time,	she	would	volunteer	every day.
	people	didn't care,	–	they	wouldn't	help.	

Questions

If-clause				Result clause				
If	Subject	Simple past		*Wh-*word	*Would / Wouldn't*	Subject	Base form of verb	
If	you	had	more money,	what	would	you	do?	
	they	had	the time,	–	would	they	help	us?

Notes

- The *if-clause* uses the simple past, but this is not a past statement. It's about the present.
- For the *be* verb, use *were* for all subjects: *If he **were** president… If they **were** free…*
- The *if-clause* can come at the beginning or end of a sentence. Use a comma when the *if-clause* comes at the beginning of a sentence.

Affirmative statements			Negative statements				
Subject	*Have to / Need to*	Base form of verb	Subject	*Do / Does*	*Not*	*Have to / Need to*	Base form of verb
I	**have to**	**make** photocopies.	I	**do**	**not**	**have to**	**make** photocopies.
He	**has to**		He	**does**			
She	**needs to**	**order** lunch.	She	**does**		**need to**	**order** lunch.
They	**need to**		They	**do**			

Yes / No question				Short answers	
Do	Subject	*Have to / Need to*	Base form of verb	Affirmative	Negative
Do	I	**have to**	**be** there early?	Yes, you **do**.	No, you **don't**.

Information question					Answer		
Wh-word	*Do*	Subject	*Have to / Need to*	Base form of verb	Subject	*Have to / Need to*	Base form of verb
What	**do**	we	**need to**	**bring**?	You	**need to**	**bring** your laptops.

Phrasal verbs are made up of a verb + particle. Particles look like prepositions (*with*, *of*, *on*), but together with the verb they have a different meaning.

Separable phrasal verbs								
Subject	Verb	Particle	Object		Subject	Verb	Object	Particle
I	**put**	**together**	a plan.	or	I	**put**	a plan	**together**.
Arun	**backs**	**up**	the files.		Arun	**backs**	them	**up**.

Inseparable phrasal verbs			
Subject	Verb	Particle	Object
Mira	**is getting**	**on**	the Internet.
We	**went**	**over**	the notes.

Notes
- With separable phrasal verbs, the object can come before or after the particle.
- When the object is a pronoun, it ***must*** come after the verb and before the particle. Compare these examples:
  *I put **a plan** together.*   *I put **it** together.*
  *I put together **a plan**.*   **NOT**   ~~I put together it.~~
- With **inseparable** phrasal verbs, the object always comes after the particle.
  *We went over **the notes**.*   *We went over **them**.*

Inseparable phrasal verbs

agree with	come by	get by	go over	make up	speak up
back out	count on	get in	hang out	meet up	talk over
come across	disagree with	get out	hear from	run into	turn into
come along	get ahead	go for	hold on	show up	watch out

Separable phrasal verbs

break down	figure out	keep up	put down	throw away	turn off
call off	fill in	look up	put off	throw out	turn on
check out	fill out	pick out	put on	try on	turn over
cheer up	give back	pick up	set up	try out	use up
clean up	give up	point out	shut off	turn around	wear out
cross out	hang up	put away	think over	turn down	write down

Three-word phrasal verbs

break up with	come down with	get along with	look out for	run out of
catch up on	come up with	keep up with	look up to	stand up for
catch up with	get around to	look down on	make up for	stand up to
check up on	get away with	look forward to	put up with	take care of

IRREGULAR VERBS

Base form of verb	Simple past	Past participle	Base form of verb	Simple past	Past participle
be	was	been	leave	left	left
become	became	become	lay (off)	laid (off)	laid (off)
begin	began	begun	lose	lost	lost
break	broke	broken	make	made	made
bring	brought	brought	mean	meant	meant
build	built	built	meet	met	met
buy	bought	bought	oversleep	overslept	overslept
catch	caught	caught	pay	paid	paid
choose	chose	chosen	put	put	put
come	came	come	quit	quit	quit
cut	cut	cut	read	read	read
cost	cost	cost	ride	rode	ridden
deal	dealt	dealt	rise	rose	risen
do	did	done	run	run	run
draw	drew	drawn	say	said	said
drink	drank	drunk	see	saw	seen
drive	drove	driven	sell	sold	sold
eat	ate	eaten	send	sent	sent
fall	fell	fallen	set	set	set
feed	fed	fed	show	showed	shown
feel	felt	felt	shut	shut	shut
fight	fought	fought	sing	sang	sung
find	found	found	sit	sit	sit
fly	flew	flown	sleep	slept	slept
forget	forgot	forgotten	speak	spoke	spoken
forgive	forgave	forgiven	spend	spent	spent
freeze	froze	frozen	stand	stood	stood
get	got	gotten	steal	stole	stolen
give	gave	given	swim	swam	swum
go	went	gone	take	took	taken
grow	grew	grown	teach	taught	taught
have	had	had	tell	told	told
hear	heard	heard	think	thought	thought
hide	hid	hidden	understand	understood	understood
hit	hit	hit	wear	wore	worn
hold	held	held	win	won	won
know	knew	known	write	wrote	written

about	below	from...to	outside
above	beneath	in	over
across	beside	in front of	past
after	besides	inside	round / around
against	between	in spite of	since
ahead of	beyond	into	than
along	but	like	through
among	by	near	throughout
apart from	concerning	next to	to
around	despite	of	towards
as	down	off	under
at	during	on	until
away from	except (for)	onto	up
because of	facing	on top of	with
before	for	opposite	within
behind	from	out of	without

METRIC CONVERSIONS

Volume		Length and distance		Weight	
1 fluid ounce	29.57 milliliters	1 centimeter	.39 inch	1 ounce	28.35 grams
1 milliliter	.034 fluid ounce	1 inch	2.54 centimeters	1 gram	.04 ounce
1 pint	.47 liter	1 foot	.30 meter	1 pound	.45 kilogram
1 liter	2.11 pints	1 meter	3.28 feet	1 kilogram	2.2 pounds
1 quart	.95 liter	1 yard	.91 meter		
1 liter	1.06 quarts	1 meter	1.09 yards		
1 gallon	3.79 liters	1 mile	1.61 kilometers		
1 liter	.26 gallon	1 kilometer	.62 mile		

THE WRITING PROCESS

The writing process consists of 5 stages:

1. Pre-writing
2. Drafting
3. Revising
4. Proofreading
5. Publishing

The five stages of the writing process can be applied to any type of writing task. Whether you are writing an essay, an article, or a blog entry, each stage allows your writing to progress from an idea in your head to a completed text. With each stage you shape and improve your writing.

Pre-writing	**PLAN**
	⇨ The Pre-writing stage is where you make a plan for your writing.
	⇨ Choose a topic you want to write about.
	⇨ Think about what you want to say about the topic.
	⇨ Generate ideas using brainstorming techniques (mind maps, idea webs, lists, etc.).
	⇨ Do research, if necessary, and take notes.
	⇨ Use graphic organizers and charts to start arranging your ideas.
Drafting	**WRITE**
	⇨ The Drafting stage is where you begin to turn your ideas into a written text.
	⇨ Think about your audience. Your tone will vary if you are writing for students or business professionals or to a friend or a university professor.
	⇨ Use ideas from the Pre-writing stage to start composing sentences and paragraphs. Don't focus too much on grammar and mechanics. Just get ideas flowing.
	⇨ If using researched materials, put the information in your own words or use quotations. Keep track of the references you use.
	⇨ First focus on the body of your text. Then add a beginning and ending.
	⇨ Read your draft to see if what you're saying flows logically.
	⇨ You may need to complete this stage more than once.
Revising	**IMPROVE**
	⇨ The Revising stage helps you to improve tone, content, style, and organization.
	⇨ Consider your target audience again and adjust the tone as needed.
	⇨ Cut, add, change, and rearrange text as needed.
	⇨ Develop an effective beginning and ending.
	⇨ Check if you need to give more information about any details.
	⇨ Vary words that you repeat too often.
	⇨ Revisit the drafting steps to develop new ideas that need to be added.
	⇨ Ask a friend or classmate to review your draft, and incorporate feedback that you find helpful.
	⇨ Set your writing aside and then return to it with fresh eyes and read it again.
	⇨ You may need to complete this stage more than once.

Proofreading	**CORRECT** ⇨ The Proofreading stage comes only after you are happy with tone, content, style, and organization. ⇨ Print your document before proofreading if you are working on a computer. You may notice mistakes that you can miss on a screen. ⇨ Look for errors in spelling, punctuation, and capitalization. Read your text several times, first focusing only on spelling, then on punctuation, then on capitalization. ⇨ Do several sweeps for grammar mistakes, checking for your individual problem areas. For example, first focus on sentence structure, then read again to check for subject-verb agreement, then again for use of tenses. ⇨ Check that you listed any references correctly. ⇨ Ask another person to proofread your text for you. Make sure you agree with the corrections and understand them before applying them. ⇨ Once you print a final copy, don't add hand-written corrections. Print a clean copy.
Publishing	**SHARE** ⇨ Finally, at the Publishing stage, you can share your text with other people. ⇨ Post it online. ⇨ Send it in an email or letter. ⇨ Present it orally to people. ⇨ Hand it in to a teacher or supervisor. ⇨ Submit it to a publication or a contest.

PRESENTATION SELF-EVALUATION

Fill out the evaluation after giving your presentation. If possible, ask a classmate to record your presentation. Then complete the chart after watching it. Be honest and keep notes of your observations to improve future presentations.

Criteria	Goals	Self rating 1–4 4 Excellent 3 Good 2 Fair 1 Poor	Room for improvement
ORGANIZATION	I planned and researched my topic well.		
PRESENTATION SKILLS	I incorporated tips from the Presentation Skill box in my preparation.		
FLOW OF IDEAS	My ideas flowed logically, and I stayed on topic.		
PREPAREDNESS	I was well prepared. It was obvious I had practiced enough.		
DELIVERY	I spoke clearly and loudly enough so everyone could easily understand me.		
BODY LANGUAGE	I held the audience's attention with varied gestures and eye contact.		
CONFIDENCE	I was relaxed and spoke with ease and enthusiasm.		
VISUAL AIDS	I incorporated visual aids and used them effectively.		
TIME	I spoke within the two-minute time frame.		
RESPONSE TO AUDIENCE	I was able to effectively answer questions and respond to comments.		

StartUp Level 5 SB Photo Credits

Cover

Liyao Xie/Moment/Getty Images (front); Tovovan/Shutterstock (back).

To the Teacher

Page ix: (Leti Molina) Pearson Education Inc.; ix (pouring): Lars Christensen/Shutterstock; ix (drizzling): Marie Martin/Shutterstock; ix (humid): Feellgood/123RF; ix (freezing): Nobilior/123RF; ix (hailing): Surne1shots/Shutterstock; ix (overcast): Zoran Photographer/Shutterstock; ix (soaked): Sun ok/Shutterstock; ix (sunburned): Graphbottles/Shutterstock; ix (damaged): Nightman1965/123RF; ix (stuck): Oleg1824/Shutterstock; ix (Leti and Marco sitting): Pearson Education Inc.; ix (elephants): W. Perry Conway/Corbis/Getty Images; ix (Leti and Marco from MyEnglish Lab): Pearson Education Inc.; ix (bottom): G-stockstudio/Shutterstock.

Welcome Unit

Page 2 (1): Shutterstock; 2 (2): Shutterstock; 2 (3): DGLimages/Shutterstock; 2 (4): Undrey/Shutterstock; 2 (5): Barock/Shutterstock; 2 (6): Air Images/Shutterstock; 3: Liyao Xie/Moment/Getty Images; 4: Pearson Education Inc.

Unit 1

Page 5 (elephants): W. Perry Conway/Corbis/Getty Images; 5 (Leti Molina): Pearson Education Inc.; 6 (Leti Molina): Pearson Education Inc.; 6 (pouring): Lars Christensen/Shutterstock; 6 (drizzling): Marie Martin/Shutterstock; 6 (humid): Feellgood/123RF; 6 (soaked): Sun ok/Shutterstock; 6 (sunburned): Graphbottles/Shutterstock; 6 (freezing): Nobilior/123RF; 6 (hailing): Surne1shots/Shutterstock; 6 (overcast): Zoran Photographer/Shutterstock; 6 (damaged): Nightman1965/123RF; 6 (stuck): Oleg1824/Shutterstock; 7: Pearson Education Inc.; 8 (Leti Molina): Pearson Education Inc.; 8 (elephant): Michael Potter11/Shutterstock; 8 (lion): Byrdyak/123RF; 8 (snake): Paytai/Shutterstock; 8 (bat): Independent birds/Shutterstock; 8 (hippopotamus): Adwo/Shutterstock; 8 (blue whale): Andrew Sutton/Shutterstock; 8 (tarantula): Cathy Keifer/Shutterstock; 9: Pearson Education Inc.; 10 (Leti Molina): Pearson Education Inc.; 10 (1): Tatyana Aleksieva-Sabeva/123RF; 10 (2): Matyas Rehak/123RF; 10 (3): Oticki/Shutterstock; 10 (4): Natalia Pascari/123RF; 10 (5): Jonathan Vasata/123RF; 10 (6): Arangan Ananth/Shutterstock; 10 (7): Ng Yin Jian/Shutterstock; 10 (8): Zeljko Radojko/Shutterstock; 11: Pearson Education Inc.; 12 (Leti Molina): Pearson Education Inc.; 12 (sloth): Ignasi Such/123RF; 12 (Howler Monkey) Jaana Piira/Shutterstock; 12 (porcupine): Jan Csernoch/Alamy Stock Photo; 14 (Leti Molina): Pearson Education Inc.; 14 (surfing): David McShane/123RF; 14 (flowers): Pittaya Phetphu/123RF; 14 (fried plantains): Ildipapp/123RF; 16: Jan-Dirk Hansen/123RF.

Unit 2

Page 17: Chris Ryan/OJO Images/Getty Images; 17 (Ed Miller): Pearson Education Inc.; 18 (Ed Miller): Pearson Education Inc.; 18 (center, right): Pixsooz/Shutterstock; 19: Pearson Education Inc.; 20: Pearson Education Inc.; 21: Pearson Education Inc.; 22: Pearson Education Inc.; 23: Pearson Education Inc.; 24 (Ed Miller): Pearson Education Inc.; 24 (center, right): Shutterstock; 26 (Ed Miller): Pearson Education Inc.; 26 (woman thinking): Minerva Studio/Shutterstock; 28: Amble Design/Shutterstock.

Unit 3

Page 29: Aluxum/iStock/Getty Images; 29 (Paula Florez): Pearson Education Inc.; 30 (Paula Florez): Pearson Education Inc.; 30 (concert): Goran Djukanovic/Shutterstock; 30 (magic show): Vchal/Shutterstock; 30 (puppet show): MilousSK/Shutterstock; 30 (food fair): Alexey Borodin/Shutterstock; 30 (art exhibit): Africa Studio/Shutterstock; 30 (fireworks): Gino Santa Maria/Shutterstock; 30 (baking contest): Dennis Gottlieb/Photodisc/Getty images; 30 (carnival): Annette Shaff/Shutterstock; 30 (parade): Operation Shooting/Shutterstock; 30 (race): Hero Images/Getty Images; 31: Pearson Education Inc.; 32 (Paula Florez): Pearson Education Inc.; 32 (center, left): Javi_Indy/Shutterstock; 33: Pearson Education Inc.; 34 (Paula Florez): Pearson Education Inc.; 34 (center): Rawpixel/123RF; 35: Pearson Education Inc.; 36 (Paula Florez): Pearson Education Inc.; 36 (railway): Evaldo Rossi/EyeEm/Getty Images; 36 (knitting): Vitalij Sova/123RF; 38 (Paula Florez): Pearson Education Inc.; 38 (dinosaur): Tvamvakinos/Shutterstock; 38 (concert): Zeljkodan/Shutterstock; 38 (farmer's market): Mangostock/Shutterstock; 40: Leonardo Munoz/EPA/Shutterstock.

Unit 4

Page 41: Svetikd/E+/Getty images; 41 (Lan Pham): Pearson Education Inc.; 42: Pearson Education Inc.; 43: Pearson Education Inc.; 44: Pearson Education Inc.; 45: Pearson Education Inc.; 46: Pearson Education Inc.; 47: Pearson Education Inc.; 48 (Lan Pham): Pearson Education Inc.; 48 (Camera): Lukas Gojda/123RF; 48 (tea set): Tadeusz Wejkszo/123RF; 48 (paper crown): Andriy Sarymsakov/123RF; 50 (Lan Pham): Pearson Education Inc.; 50 (center): Ruslan Kudrin/Alamy Stock Photo; 50 (bottom): Dejan Jekic/Alamy Stock Photo; 52: Beephoto/123RF.

Unit 5

Page 53: Andresr/E+/Getty Images; 53 (Ahmet Tanir): Pearson Education Inc.; 54 (Ahmet Tanir): Pearson Education Inc.; 54 (soda can): Weiloong/123RF; 54 (exercise): Maridav/Shutterstock; 54 (drink water): Ferli/123RF; 54 (sleep): Shutterstock; 54 (meditation): Luckybusiness/123RF; 54 (doctor checkup): Rocketclips/Shutterstock; 54 (healty food): Jacek Chabraszewski/Shutterstock; 54 (hike in nature): CreativeDoctah/Shutterstock; 55: Pearson Education Inc.; 56 (Ahmet Tanir): Pearson Education Inc.; 56 (feet ache): Sirinapa/123RF; 56 (pulled muscle): Toa55/Shutterstock; 56 (swollen ankles): Lavizzara/Shutterstock; 56 (sore back): Andriy Popov/123RF; 56 (sprained wrist): Decade3d/123RF; 56 (hurt knee): Izf/Shutterstock; 56 (exhausted): Racorn/123RF; 56 (sore throat): Gstockstudio/123RF; 56 (broken thumb): Dorling Kindersley/Getty Images; 56 (stiff neck): Szefei/123RF; 57: Pearson Education Inc.; 58: Pearson Education Inc.; 59: Pearson Education Inc.; 60 (Ahmet Tanir): Pearson Education Inc.; 60 (Yuzuru Hanyu): Aflo/Shutterstock; 60 (Serena Williams): Jimmie48 Photography/Shutterstock; 60 (Lionel Messi): Ververidis Vasilis/Shutterstock; 62 (Ahmet Tanir): Pearson Education Inc.; 62 (center, left): Shutterstock; 64: Dolgachov/123RF.

Unit 6

Page 65: Luka Lajst/E+/Getty Images; 65 (Marcos Alves): Pearson Education Inc.; 66 (Marcos Alves): Pearson Education Inc.; 66 (Mona Lisa): GL Archive/Alamy Stock Photo; 66 (Great Train Robbery): Monty Fresco/Associated Newspapers/Shutterstock; 66 (John Paul Getty III): Crollalanza/Shutterstock; 66 (Jack the Ripper): Historia/Shutterstock; 67: Pearson Education Inc.; 68: Pearson Education Inc.; 69: Pearson Education Inc.; 70 (Marcos Alves) Pearson Education Inc.; 70 (blood stain): Oxana Bernatskaya/123RF; 70 (DNA): Sergey Nivens/123RF; 70 (fingerprint): PRILL/Shutterstock; 70 (bullet): Charnsit Ramyarupa/123RF; 70 (investigator): Edw/Shutterstock; 70 (bullet hole): Steve Collender/123RF; 70 (wound): Tobkatrina/Shutterstock; 70 (bruise): Lzflzf/123RF; 71: Pearson Education Inc.; 72 (Marcos Alves): Pearson Education Inc.; 72 (center, right): Pictorial Press Ltd/Alamy Stock Photo; 73: Galina Peshkova/123RF; 74 (Marcos Alves): Pearson Education Inc.; 74 (center, right): Milosz Aniol/123RF; 75: Tero Vesalainen/Shutterstock; 76: Nick Starichenko/Shutterstock.

Unit 7

Page 77: Devon Strong/The Image Bank/Getty Images; 77 (Ed Miller): Pearson Education Inc.; 78 (Ed Miller): Pearson Education Inc.; 78 (zip up): Svetlana Cherkasova/Shutterstock; 78 (take off): Cecilia Tomio/Shutterstock; 78 (put on): Galina Tcivina/Shutterstock; 78 (tie): Dmytro Panchenko/123RF; 78 (button): Moodboard/123RF; 78 (tight t-shirt): Alan poulson/123RF; 78 (loose shirt): Alexandr Bognat/123RF; 78 (long-sleeved): Dmitry Naumov/123RF; 78 (short-sleeved): Ptnphoto/123RF; 78 (sleeveless): Ludmila Baryshnikova/123RF; 78 (floral): Federico Cimino/123RF; 78 (stripped): Aleksandr Belugin/123RF; 78 (plaid): Ruth Black/123RF; 78 (polka-dotted): Aleksandr Prokopenko/123RF; 78 (solid blue): Sorapong Chaipanya/123RF; 79: Pearson Education Inc.; 79 (left, room background): Africa Studio/Shutterstock; 79 (right, room background): Anna Maksimyuk/Shutterstock; 80: Pearson Education Inc.; 81: Pearson Education Inc.; 82: Pearson Education Inc.; 83: Pearson Education Inc.; 84 (Ed Miller): Pearson Education Inc.; 84 (center, left): Dmitriy Shironosov/123RF; 85: Olena Kachmar/123RF; 86 (Ed Miller): Pearson Education Inc.; 86 (man, Mateo Diaz): Katarzyna Bialasiewicz/123RF; 86 (woman, Kristen Walters): Anna Furman/123RF; 88: Dolgachov/123RF.

Unit 8

Page 89: Zapp2Photo/Shutterstock; 89 (Paula Florez): Pearson Education Inc.; 90 (Paula Florez): Pearson Education Inc.; 90 (code): Nd3000/Shutterstock; 90 (software): Ian Wedgewood/Pearson Education Ltd; 90 (apps): Georgejmclittle/123RF; 90 (virus): Georgejmclittle/123RF; 90 (network): Oleksiy Mark/Shutterstock; 90 (hardware): Auremar/123RF; 91: Pearson Education Inc.; 92: Pearson Education Inc.; 93: Pearson Education Inc.; 94: Pearson Education Inc.; 95: Pearson Education Inc.; 96: Pearson Education Inc.; 98 Pearson Education Inc.; 98 (center. right): Victor Habbick Visions/Science Photo Library/Alamy Stock Photo; 99: Gorodenkoff/Shutterstock; 100: Panuwat Phimpha/Shutterstock.

Unit 9

Page 101: Rawpixel.com/Shutterstock; 101 (Lan Pham): Pearson Education Inc.; 102 (Lan Pham): Pearson Education Inc.; 102 (maintenance staff): ALPA PROD/Shutterstock; 102 (security personal): FangXiaNuo/E+/Getty Images; 102 (greeter): Wavebreak Media Ltd/Getty Images; 102 (waitstaff): Albert Yuralaits/123RF; 102 (caterer): Wavebreakmedia/Shutterstock; 102 (presenter): Kasto/123RF; 102 (supervisor): Golubovy/123RF; 102 (tech support): Tyler Olson/123RF; 103: Pearson Education Inc.; 104 (Lan Pham): Pearson Education Inc.; 104 (make agreement): Asdf_Media/Shutterstock; 104 (sign contract): Thodonal/123RF; 104 (cancel agreement): Uladzislau Salikhau/123RF; 104 (accept offer): UfaBizPhoto/Shutterstock; 104 (reject offer): FangXiaNuo/E+/Getty Images; 104 (make suggestion): Zoriana Zaitseva/Shutterstock; 104 (offer lower rate): Kurhan/Shutterstock; 104 (walk away): Bbtreesubmission/123RF; 105: Pearson Education Inc.; 106: Pearson Education Inc.; 107: Pearson Education Inc.; 108 (Lan Pham): Pearson Education Inc.; 108 (center, left): Aleksandr Davydov/123RF; (center, right) Dmitriy Shironosov/123RF; 110 (Lan Pham): Pearson Education Inc.; 110 (woman, Ask Ana): Rick Gomez/Getty Images; 110 (women on sofa): Weedezign/iStock/Getty Images; 111: AJR_photo/Shutterstock.

Unit 10

Page 113: Vchal/Shutterstock; 113 (Ed Miller): Pearson Education Inc.; 114 (Ed Miller): Pearson Education Inc.; 114 (excuse): Avid_creative/E+/Getty Images; 114 (suggestion): Dmitry Kalinovsky/123RF; 114 (idea): UM-UMM/Shutterstock; 114 (explanation): Dolgachov/123RF; 114 (disagreement): Roman Kosolapov/Shutterstock; 114 (complaint): Elnur Amikishiyev/123RF; 114 (point): Moodboard/123RF; 115: Pearson Education Inc.; 116: Pearson Education Inc.; 117: Pearson Education Inc.; 118 (Ed Miller): Pearson Education Inc.; 118 (prisoner escape): LightField Studios/Shutterstock; 118 (students surprised): Antonio Guillem/123RF; 118 (respectful to grandmother): Toa55/Shutterstock; 118 (sympathetic nurse): ERproductions Ltd/DigitalVision/Getty Images; 118 (comforting to child): Vyacheslav Volkov/123RF; 118 (demanding child): Kenishirotie/123RF; 118 (unreasonable child): Dmytro Zinkevych/123RF; 118 (emotional man): ESB Professional/Shutterstock; 119: Pearson Education Inc.; 120 (Ed Miller): Pearson Education Inc.; 120 (family): Ideabug/E+/Getty Images; 120 (vaccinating child): Valeriya Anufriyeva/Shutterstock; 121: FocusStocker/Shutterstock; 122 (Ed Miller): Pearson Education Inc.; 122 (center): Rawpixel/123RF; 124: Olena Yakobchuk/123RF.

Grammar Practice /Vocabulary Practice

Page 125: Steve Debenport/E+/Getty Images; 126: Yuliya Ozeran/Shutterstock; 128: Mark Bowden/123RF; 129: Gordana Sermek/Shutterstock; 131: Gino Santa Maria/Shutterstock; 132: Kzenon/123RF; 134: Karkas/Shutterstock; 135: Allesalltag/Alamy Stock Photo; 137: Dean Drobot/Shutterstock; 138: Wavebreak Media Ltd/Shutterstock; 140: Pedro Valdez/Cultura RM/Alamy Stock Photo; 141: Digital Storm/Shutterstock; 143: Jassada Watt/Shutterstock; 144: Michael Warwick/Shutterstock; 146: Elnur Amikishiyev/123RF; 147: William Perugini/Shutterstock; 149: Ammentorp/123RF; 150: Wavebreak Media Ltd/123RF; 152: Dolgachov/123RF; 153: Mangostar/Shutterstock.

Illustration Credits

418 Neal (KJA Artists), John Goodwin (Eye Candy Illustration)